FAKING IT

FAKING IT

A Look into the Mind of
a Creative Learner

Christopher M. Lee
and
Rosemary F. Jackson

BOYNTON/COOK PUBLISHERS
HEINEMANN
Portsmouth, NH

BOYNTON/COOK PUBLISHERS
A Subsidiary of
HEINEMANN EDUCATIONAL BOOKS, INC.
361 Hanover Street, Portsmouth, NH 03801-3959
Offices and agents throughout the world

Library of Congress Cataloging-in-Publication Data

Lee, Christopher M.
    Faking it : a look into the mind of a creative learner /
Christopher M. Lee and Rosemary F. Jackson.
        p.   cm.
    ISBN 0-86709-296-3
    1. Lee, Christopher M.   2. Learning disabled—United States—
Biography.   3. Creative thinking.   4. Self-confidence.
I. Jackson, Rosemary F.   II. Title.
LC4705.L44   1992
371.9—dc20   91-23844
                                                                      CIP

Interior design by Jenny Jensen Greenleaf.
Printed in the United States of America.
92 93 94 95 96 9 8 7 6 5 4 3 2

A unique bond connects my sister, brother, and me. We all have creative ways of looking at life. It is as if we are one being which possesses spontaneousness, recklessness, and seriousness all at once. With love and creativity, I dedicate this book to the best parts of me, spontaneousness and recklessness, Michelle and Craig Lee.

In Memory of
Jimi

A friend to all, special to me
Jimi was unpredictable, and carefree
With grace of movement from sea to sea
A dolphin
yearning to be free

Leaving a wake, stirring all who pass
The secret of life within her grasp
Always seeming to know the answers
Even before the questions asked

No longer confined to human form
A spirit freed
She left her energy with me

CONTENTS

Preface   ix

Acknowledgments   xv

Introduction   xvii

Chapter 1: Uncovering Your Potential   1

Chapter 2: Faking It   7

Chapter 3: Writing: My Worst Nightmare   21

Chapter 4: Reading: Making the Words Come Alive   39

Chapter 5: Language: Making It Real   59

Chapter 6: Math: A Different Language System   85

Chapter 7: Private Pain   101

Chapter 8: A New Beginning   143

Afterword: Rosemary's Turn   145

Appendix 1: Regents' Essay   175

Appendix 2: Sample Essay not Using Computer   177

Appendix 3: Journal Entry, Freshman Year   179

Appendix 4: Journal Entry, Freshman Year   181
             (cursive writing sample)

PREFACE

Rosemary F. Jackson

In 1986, I was working as a doctoral assistant in the University of Georgia Learning Disabilities Adult Clinic. Christopher Lee, a freshman who had just been evaluated by the clinic, was assigned to me as my first student/ client. At our first meeting, Chris was extremely resistant —I represented the academic world he had battled all his life, an incomprehensible SYSTEM that hovered over him as the oppressive enemy which had imprisoned him in a world of false self-perceptions. He saw me not as a tutor but as a prison guard. In our first consultation (confrontation) his eyes fixed directly on the pictures that lined the wall behind me. His hands were drained of color as they gripped the arms of the chair he had locked himself into. There was no warmth, no spark, only animosity for the system he believed did not work.

As months and then quarters went by, I slowly introduced Chris into a new system, one that emphasized strengths rather than weaknesses. As he gained trust in me, he gained confidence in himself. The years went by and our relationship grew just as Chris's faith did in me and our clinic. As Chris approached his last year in school, not only had he accepted his learning difficulties, he had also grown to a point where he wanted to help others. He had a story to tell, the story of a boy who had no belief in his own abilities because of the system, now a young man who wanted to change that system.

The book that follows is that story. It was written over the period of one year, Chris's last at the University of

Georgia. He had completed four years of his swimming eligibility, but had one year remaining to complete his degree requirements. What was left to do with all that extra time but to write a book?

When school began that fall, we set aside Wednesday nights as our night to write. We worked in my office on the same computer on which we had struggled through class papers for four years. It was a comfortable setting, and we were comfortable with each other. Starting around five o'clock, we would begin talking about a particular topic until the talking progressed into putting something down on paper. We agreed to make notes during the week about ideas or examples that came to mind, and invariably we found that a theme had developed from one Wednesday to the next. At first we stuck to what we had agreed beforehand to write about, but we found later that it was best to write about whatever was on Chris's mind that particular Wendesday night.

The work was difficult, in part because we were defining and redefining our intentions and goals as we went along, and in part because it was hard for Chris to go back into his childhood to recover and recount some very painful memories. The writing itself is, for me, and I hope for others, an instructive example of how an unusual kind of collaboration can blossom into a powerful example of individual art. Although Chris wrote some of the passages in this book totally on his own, we wrote most of it as a team. *All* of the words and ideas are his; I simply asked the questions and typed his responses verbatim. We would then go over the passages again and again until he got them just the way he wanted them. He would often have me read a passage to him several times, focusing each time on a particular word or phrase which did not suit him exactly. (*There—that sentence right there. Every time you read it, you stumble over the words. We've got to make that read smoother.*)

When I remember the freshman swimmer who had such language problems, I am amazed at Chris's command of language. Once he understood that language as a whole was a problem, he set out to conquer it one word at a time. When we began writing this book, the writing itself was more of a team effort. Chris would often start a sentence and I would finish it. As the work progressed, however, Chris gradually took command of the writing until he took over completely. I continued to ask questions and let him know when he was not getting his ideas across clearly, but my job became more that of secretary and editor. I took down his thoughts in his words and made sure the words were spelled correctly. We worked in a disorganized manner, jotting down thoughts on various topics at various times. I would then organize the pieces into chapter form, and together we would work on the "feel" of the chapter as a whole. (When I wrote the Afterword totally on my own, I felt somewhat inadequate without my partner around to provide the words I wanted to use. Talk about role reversal!)

The Introduction and Chapters 1–8, the heart (and soul) of the book, comprise Chris's story—how he came to be, and see himself as, a "creative learner." The Afterword is mine, recounting how I wound up in the Learning Disabilities Adult Clinic and how we work in the Clinic with a variety of creative learners whose gumption got them to the University of Georgia in the first place.

There were many times over the year we worked on the book that the writing got very serious and emotions ran high. At other times we became unbelievably silly. We always ordered pizza around 6:30 and took a break just to chat. Now that we are living in separate cities with new job responsibilities, we each still get a craving around 6:30 every Wednesday to send out for pizza and call each other on the phone. We hope you enjoy reading this book as much as we enjoyed writing it and have enjoyed living with it ever since.

ACKNOWLEDGMENTS

A shell waits on a beach to be carried out into the unknown, fragile in form, confused with color, desperate to be noticed. People pass by inattentive to the shells being crushed beneath their feet. Occasionally, special individuals pause, pick up the shell and study it. They notice the form, the color, the smell, the texture. They take the time to enjoy it instead of walking by. These people are as unique as the shells they touch, for they have given the gifts of time and awareness. We have been lucky, for we have not been passed by. These are the individuals who took the time to notice. Thank you, for your time was not wasted.

Don Jackson
Kathy and Mike Lee
K.K., Nana, & Papa
Michelle & Craig Lee
The UGA Learning Disabilities Adult Clinic
Noël Gregg
Diane Wahlers
Donald Lyman
Beth Baily
Vicki Martin
Margo Habiger
Cheri Hoy
Jimi Brockmeyer
Robert Woodruff
Donnie Dicer

Pam Brown
Cathy Chase
Kristin Sandercock
Jennifer Morton
Carey Davis

To the teachers who made a difference:
Amelia Davis Horne
Hyta Mederer
Chris Hays
JoAnne Juett
Marshall Darley

A special thanks to Bob Boynton for having the faith
and foresight to turn our vision into reality.

INTRODUCTION

I am told that I have a learning disability. However, this book is not about a person who has a learning disability. It is the story of a creative learner—one who has been given the *label* "learning disabled." I am not a professional educator and this is my book, and I will not think of myself as disabled in any way. "Disability" is defined by *The American Heritage Desk Dictionary* as "the condition of lacking a physical or mental capacity." Ask yourself, what images are formed by the definition? Am I intelligent or dumb? Am I tall or short? Strong or weak? Secure or insecure? Do I play the role of an outcast? There is no doubt about what images are drawn, what figure is seen. The definition provokes an image of inferiority, one a child would carry throughout life. In reading this book, you will see that this image is false. However, it has taken supportive parents, a few creative teachers, and lots of work on my part to undo the negative effects of the label that was given to me by the education system.

I believe that the label "learning disabled" automatically cripples children and places them in the back of the line. They become products of the definition. The crippling effect this label had on me is reflected in the first two chapters of this book. They are tinged with the despair I felt at the time. There is no more despair. I have learned to accept myself for who I am. I have chosen my own labels: I am a student, a writer, an athlete, and most importantly a person with only positive labels. What image is drawn now?

The purpose of this book is to inspire and motivate people who are scared of becoming the best they can be —a link that will help people connect themselves to their ambitions and uncover their potential.

Scared to try and unwilling to explore, some individuals are trapped into believing they lack potential when it is really self-confidence that is missing. This story is for those who have tried yet could not find their way, and for those who will not take the risk because of past experiences. In telling my story, I hope to inspire individuals who are hiding behind masks of negative self-concepts to face their fears, discover their strengths, and use them to overcome or bypass their weaknesses.

The label "disabled" takes away self-confidence. This book is designed to prevent the negative effects of labeling and to return this inner power to those who have learning difficulties. Because I have unique learning abilities, I have given myself an additional label—that of **creative learner**. Follow me through this book, and I will teach you the power of creative learning.

To me, self-confidence is an endless vision, and without vision, there is only an end.

ONE

Uncovering Your Potential

It is Friday afternoon, the day before a football game at the University of Georgia where I am a senior. The parking lots around the stadium are already beginning to fill with alumni dressed in red and black. They set up their campers and crank up the game day music. "Go dawgs!" rings across the campus. Some students are already putting the first mug of beer to their mouths in anticipation of tomorrow's win. I strain to concentrate amidst the excitement surrounding me. I am sitting in my room with only my botany book for company. I want to be with my friends, but I know I can't. I've covered myself. I've told them all that I am out partying. Even after four years most of them have not figured out that I really spend most of my time being tutored or studying.

In fact only a few of my friends even know I have a learning disability. Most of them will find out for the first time when they read this book. Writing this book is one of the hardest things I have ever done, not only because of the difficulty I have in putting the words to paper, but also because I have spent my entire life hiding this problem from everyone, including myself.

Admitting a problem is confronting a flaw. Confronting the flaw is confronting the consequences of imperfection. One then has to make the choice of whether to deal with the consequences or hide the flaw. Youth allows us the opportunity to face the flaw without allowing the flaw to defeat us. Young people find it easier to be con-

1

vinced that they are invincible. I know this feeling of in-vincibility. I have felt it myself. Young people feel they can do anything, but so often they don't fulfill their potential because they have no guidance. For someone with a learning disability to master the disability, he or she must have guidance in facing the problems and dealing with them. Through this book I hope to help people—parents and teachers, as well as creative learners—understand what it is truly like to be a student with unique learning abilities. By relating my experiences and my feelings, I hope to help individuals who have unique learning abilities face their problems and conquer them, while at the same time help give a sense of guidance to those in the position to help.

Individuals with learning disabilities first need to confront and deal with their problems. A boat that has a hole in it will sink, unless the hole is patched. Facing a learning disability can be compared to patching a boat; unless the individual faces the problem and deals with it, he or she will sink. And the sooner the hole is patched, the less damage is done. The solution is not easy, however. What kind of pain does that person have to suffer and how long it will take to patch that hole are questions that are painful to ask and not easy to answer. People with physical disabilities have no choice but to face the reality of their disability. It is much easier for problems of creative learners to go unnoticed by others. Since the creative learner's handicap is inside, in the brain, other people may never realize that it exists. Students with learning disabilities can slowly sink into the background and settle for second best. They settle for being at the bottom of the sea instead of floating at the top.

I decided to write this book because I know how frustrating it is to grow up with a learning disability. I know what it is like to grow up thinking you are stupid. I now know I'm not stupid, and I want you to know how I came to this point. It has been extremely difficult for me to unravel all these years of hiding my problems and my anger. Writing this book has dredged up memories I had deeply buried simply as a means of survival. At different times during the writing of this book I have felt anger at my parents, my teachers, and particularly at the school system. And I have been far more angry at myself than at any of these people. Worse than the anger has been the disappointment I have felt in not being perfect and in knowing that I never can be. Just as a child feels safer in the dark with a sheet over his or her head, I felt safer in a classroom with an invisible mask over my face. I felt that hiding my problems would make them go away.

When I started writing this book, I was angry with myself because I realized the harm I had done to myself by wearing that mask. I later transferred my anger to the people who never saw the real me behind the mask. I was angry that I was able to get through the entire education system without anyone even knowing I had the mask on. I am still angry that people are graduating from high school every year with learning problems that have not been recognized or faced. I realize now that parents, students, and teachers must accept the responsibility for this. People with creative learning abilities are bright and inventive. Instead of learning the academics of school, they often spend their school years learning the art of conning. They find creative ways to avoid learning, and in doing so, avoid confronting their problems. Students with learning disabilities must learn to be honest with themselves and allow the teachers to see through their masks.

I guess we can never foresee the path that life will lead us down. To me it is as if people are issued certain tools which they are allowed to use throughout their lives. Over the years these tools become a part of a person's personality. We have to use them to help ourselves rather than let them weigh us down. I feel that it all comes down to how we use these tools to construct our lives. We are limited to the tools we have, so we have to use them carefully and wisely. But it is the way in which we use the tools we are given that makes us individuals. Some people are gifted with intelligence, while others are gifted athletically. Some people are poets while others are scientists. What is important is that we do the best we can with the tools we have rather than make excuses because "our" tools do not work properly. The tools that may at first appear to be useless or unmanageable can often be made to be useful if they are acknowledged and confronted. For example, it would be easy for me to run away from writing this book. But over the last two years—for the first time in my life—I find it harder and harder to run. I have learned that running away does not solve anything. I have to learn to accept the tools I have and use them to my advantage. They are *my* tools and *I* must learn to use them. I have decided to deal with and use one particular tool—my learning disability—by writing a book that might in some way be helpful.

I have been finding it harder and harder to run from my problems. I do not believe this is due to the fact that I am getting older. It's just that I find less reason to run. I could choose to continue to hide, but what benefit is there in hiding? Hiding is weak, and I am not weak. I know that all the anger that creative learners have locked up inside because of our problems gives us strength beyond imagination. I have lived with that anger. We just have to learn how to focus it. We have to use our anger to help ourselves. God knows, we have used it against ourselves long enough. Those of us who have learning differences are placed a little farther back in the race, and we have to make up some time. Even though we may fall down a few more times or find it harder to hear the lap counter, this does not mean we cannot compete in the race. We might even be able to win.

This book is long overdue. It is time for one of us creative learners to come right out and say it: We must "patch the hole in our boat," remove the mask, and allow educators in to use their knowledge to help us take advantage of the tools we are given, and focus our anger toward fighting the disability rather than letting it be a burden. Our future can be as promising as we want it to be.

TWO

Faking It

In my freshman year in college, I had a choice: either leave because I could not do the work alone or accept the fact that I needed help. I could no longer hide. My learning disabilities had finally caught up to me.

All the years of thinking I was stupid and feeling sorry for myself had also caught up with me. Even though it is very difficult for me to let down my defenses, I'm going to try to recall for you some of the things that led me to this point. I'm not trying to appeal to your sympathies. I simply want you to know where I'm coming from. In order to relate my experiences to you, you need to know a little about my life.

It was in second grade that I first realized there was something "wrong" with me. I was pulled out of the public school I attended and placed in a school for so-called "special kids." I quickly realized that the word "special" did not mean extraordinary, and in fact, did not have a positive meaning at all.

I rode a bus filled with other "special" people. Some of them were very scary because they were so physically different. One was an albino who wore thick red glasses. A few of them sat drooling in wheelchairs at the back of the bus. I sat next to the same girl every day. She had long brown hair that she wore in a ponytail. She was deaf and mute. That year she became very special to me, and even though we did not share language, we learned how to communicate. She was the one person on the bus who did not scare me. When we got to school each day, she went her way with the deaf and dumb, and I went my way

7

with the slow and stupid. I understood that I had been placed in a different environment than my friends in the neighborhood, but I did not understand why. Stupid had not entered my vocabulary yet because at this school I was normal. In fact, I was probably the most normal of the normals. The school was pretty much for problem kids. If you did not fit into the mainstream, you caused a problem, and if you caused a problem, you were placed here.

As much as this school puzzled me, I had real success here. The school seemed to ignore the academics I had struggled with the year before. Instead, we worked with our hands. It was almost as if the school was afraid to let us work with our minds. I'm not sure, but I felt like we even got longer recesses and lunches. One class that I had that none of my neighbors had was called "workshop," where we learned how to build things. It was as if I were in a vocational school for second graders. I enjoyed this class though, because I never had to use my language skills at all. It was in this class that I achieved something in school for the very first time. I have few positive memories of school before the fourth grade, but the one I remember most fondly was not a written essay or an A on a math test, but a simple stool I built in workshop. It was the first thing I felt I had ever accomplished on my own. It was real. I could touch it and sit on it and tell about it. It wasn't a meaningless story or a bunch of letters on a page someone expected me to memorize for a spelling test. It was the only thing I had ever done in school that made sense to me. I later wrote about this stool in an essay I had to write to pass the University's writing competency test, a test that must be passed to graduate from the University of Georgia (see Appendix 1).

During the summer when I was eight years old my family moved from Tallahassee to Pensacola, Florida. I remember as I left Tallahassee, sitting between my father and my brother in a big U-Haul truck, thinking that I was leaving Tallahassee having accomplished nothing. I vowed that I would come back one day and accomplish something. (In one of life's strange twists I got my second chance several years later. During my first year on the University of Georgia Swim team, I made the traveling team. One of our meets was against Florida State University *in Tallahassee*. Georgia beat FSU 65 to 60. As I left Tallahassee, this time surrounded by my teammates, I felt the sense of accomplishment that had been missing all those years ago.)

Pensacola was the time in my life between second and eighth grade. It was then that I realized for sure that I was stupid. My parents realized that the other school had not prepared me academically to face the third grade, so they decided that I should begin my school career in Pensacola by repeating the second grade. This is when I realized I was different from my classmates. During math, handwriting, and spelling, I was pulled out of my class and taken to a trailer in the back of the school where I played with blocks, word cards, and games. This was the first time I was faced with the decision to hide the fact that I was stupid or admit to it. The kids in my class were curious about why I was taken out every day. I don't remember what I told them, I just remember that I was extremely embarrassed, and this added to my feelings of stupidity. It was the first time I realized how much I really hated school and that I would never be any good at it.

My teachers were all good to me, but they were all being exposed to the concept of learning disabilities for the first time. This was 1974, the year before the Education for All Handicapped Children's Act was passed requiring that all public schools offer an appropriate education for learning disabled and other handicapped children. My teachers had heard just enough about learning disabilities to be scared of me. They turned my education over to the newly trained specialist, who knew only a little more than they did. Being sent to what my friends called the "stupid trailer" every afternoon made me feel stupid; the silly repetitious things they had me do made me feel even more stupid. I remember looking out the "stupid trailer's" window every day at recess, seeing my friends playing on the playground. Was I retarded or was I being punished? Everything was so confusing. I look back and I can see that the educational system was making an effort to help me, but no one ever sat down and talked to me about what was wrong with me. I was a kid with severe learning disabilities, but nobody ever explained this to me. My daily routine simply told me I was different, and probably stupid. I had no choice but to learn to accept the fact that I was different. By the fourth grade, I felt inferior to everybody and had learned how to keep my mouth shut.

In the fourth grade I began to learn how to hide my problems from others and run from them myself. I began to lie. I lied to my friends and to myself. I did a lot of praying even though I doubted the existence of a god who would have me live this kind of life. I wondered if I was the only one with this problem or if I was being punished for some special reason. I prayed that I would never have to read in class or answer a question aloud or participate in a spelling bee. I conveniently managed to be sick on spelling bee days.

I had great difficulty participating in the note-passing game that was so popular during this time in school. Not only could I not write notes, I had difficulty reading them too. Sometimes girls thought I didn't like them because I wouldn't answer their notes. I would smile when I got a note, trying to get by with that, because I sure couldn't get by with a pencil and paper. I wasn't learning how to deal with my problem, I was learning how to get around it. I was learning much more about hiding and conning than about reading, writing, and arithmetic. Here I was, a fourth grader, who not only hated school but hated the whole world. My opinion of myself was set for many years to come. Rather than looking forward to the future, I was afraid of everything and dreaded each day. I was nothing.

By the fifth grade I had learned how to cheat. I mastered my learning disabilities by avoiding writing or reading anything written or by cheating my way through. My teachers seemed to know something was wrong with me, and they would let me slide. My parents seemed to have endless conversations with my teachers. I was assigned extra credit work to do at home to help my grades, but I was careful to let none of my friends know about this. One day at lunch my two best friends began to pick on me about how stupid I was. I can't even remember what I had done to receive their taunts. It might have been that I had made a failing grade on an easy test or that I had pronounced something in a really funny way. Whatever it was, I knew they had finally seen through my cover. They called me stupid, and I knew I couldn't hide anymore.

I ran out of the lunchroom and away from the school. I ran over the sand dunes and onto the beach and hid and watched as the teachers came to search for me. I eventually made it home without anyone seeing me. But I had to return to the school and face my teachers and friends. This was one of the hardest things I have ever had to do. I turned within myself even more. I was careful never to make another mistake again, and I succeeded to an extent. But one more incident happened before that year was over. This time the teacher asked me to read something from the board and I couldn't read it. I don't know if I was scared or embarrassed or hurt or a mixture of all three, but I couldn't speak. I could not say one word. The whole class was staring at me. I could not read what was on the board, and I could not come up with a lie. I was faced with a classroom full of kids watching me fail, and realized that I could no longer hide the fact that I was stupid. The teacher became angry with me because she thought I was ignoring her or refusing to speak. She thought I was rebellious, the class thought I was just weird, but I knew I was only stupid.

At this time a change occurred in my life. It was a change that, in time, became necessary for my survival. Here I was in the sixth grade, stupid, scared, and weak. Other than the love from my family, I had nothing. You can only discuss sixth-grade stuff with a sixth-grade friend. So I hid. Not only was I faced with the regular pains of growing up, I had to deal with the fact that I was going to be stupid the rest of my life. I had a best friend (R-I-C-H-A-R-D. I was so proud when I learned to spell his name!) who, like everyone else, was smarter and bigger than I, although I was more intuitive than he. Richard's mom introduced us to a local swim club that was advertising for swimmers to try out. Thinking it was kind of a life-saving course, Richard and I went, not knowing how to swim. I took to it like a fish. I loved it! It gave me something to work for that was not school oriented. My dad put me on a special diet, and I started doing push-ups and sit-ups every night. I started feeling a little bit better about myself. Swimming was a good confidence builder. It became more than just a club sport. It became my life: 5:30 A.M. practices right up until school, and back to the pool again right after school. I now had a hobby that took up more than enough time and helped me to forget a little about my problems. Swimming was something I could do successfully, and because of the rigorous training schedule and the unique aspects of the sport itself, people were intrigued by my participation in it. It was something that not everybody did. I was not just another face in the crowd. I began to feel a sense of achievement and pride.

In the seventh grade I went to a small private school.

Seventh grade was possibly the best year of my school life until I got to college. It was a new start in a new school. Hiding became easier because no one knew me and because I had gotten really good at it. Swimming and running were activities that few other students participated in, and so I was set apart in a positive way and looked up to by some. The more confidence I got, the more scared I became. I was terrified that someone would find out that I couldn't spell or read and that the little bit of success I had at the time would be taken away from me. I remember one student in particular who was brighter than everyone else. She had short red hair and freckles and was very timid. She was book smart, but not people smart. I remember looking up to her and wishing I could have just a little of what she had. I had difficulty understanding why a person who was so smart seemed to lack confidence and was so uneasy around people. I watched her perform once in a "brain brawl" with other people who were just as skilled as she. I realized then that she was just as scared as I was of losing it. She was scared of not being smart one day. That's why she committed so much time to her books like I devoted so much time to swimming. It was at this time that I realized that it takes time, effort, and hard work to get something and then to hold on to it. If you want more, you have to be willing to put out the effort to get more. However, the time and effort I put into my schoolwork never seemed to be enough. I had difficulty understanding why putting in extra time worked for everything but school.

Everything seemed to be going well that year until another brick hit me in the face. I had to make a speech in class. This was the first time I was ever required to stand in front of a class and speak. Everybody hates making speeches, but for me this meant facing a problem I had managed to ignore up to this point. It was not so much the speech that concerned me; I was worried that everyone would have trouble understanding me. It was becoming clear to me that I spoke differently than everyone else. I had always been in speech classes, but so had other people. These people had always graduated from the classes, while I never did. It was always in the back of my mind that I had a speech problem, but I never really faced it until this time. I was afraid of speaking, and figured that the faster I could say what I had to, the sooner it would be over. In front of the class, without realizing it, I began rushing my words and it became more and more difficult for people to understand what I was saying. I put off the speech just as I had put off the spelling bees. I refused to go to school on the days I was supposed to give the speech. On those days my hatred of school resurfaced with a vengeance, and all my newly gained confidence evaporated. Eventually I had to give the speech. I don't know if it was my speech or my self-doubts that resulted in the poor grade, but my confidence was lost. After the speech people started asking me where I was from. Most of them thought I was from "up north" because my speech was so different from their southern drawls. Later I added their comments to my list of excuses. I began to tell people I was from New York or Boston so I would not have to explain my different speech pattern. It got to the point that I started to believe my own lies. It is funny now that I look back on it, but as a child it was easier to believe that I was from another place where everybody spoke like me. Maybe these places people were telling me I was from were full of other people just like me. I thought maybe I could go there one day and sound normal.

The rest of my high school years were spent perfecting my swimming techniques. In school I did the best that I could. I continued lying to my teachers and hiding from the same old problems. With lots of hard work I managed to get by with C's, but academics became secondary to the problems I faced in the real world. THE REAL WORLD was becoming as horrifying as school. For years my parents had taken care of my needs. But now it was time for me to assume my own responsibilities and face a new set of hurdles. They were the same hurdles I had faced all my life, but now they were at a new level, the level entitled REAL WORLD. By my sixteenth birthday I was beginning to realize what this new level involved. The first hurdle I faced was the driving test. It took me three times to pass it, and I was terrified each and every time I took it. It was as if no matter how much I studied, I could not pass the written part of the test in which I had to match up signs and words. Sure, I knew the answers, but when I had the test in front of me, it was as if it were written in a foreign language.

This ordeal was one of the worst I have ever been through. I knew I had problems in school, but it never occurred to me that I would have trouble getting a driver's license. At sixteen, a driver's license is much more than a piece of paper. It is a teenager's ticket to freedom, and I was determined not to miss out on this freedom. After I failed it the first time, my confidence was totally destroyed. As I look back on this incident, I realize how devastating it was to me. On each of the three days I took the test, the word stupid was branded deeper and deeper into my brain, and it hurt. Was it worth trying to improve myself when I had to face failure after failure? It seems so trivial now, but at the time I seriously wondered if life was worth living. I think part of my depression was the realization that this was only the *first* hurdle. There were many more to face.

The next hurdle came when my parents helped me open my own checking account. I was very excited about having the freedom and power that a checking account would bring. Like every other kid, I felt a sense of adulthood as I held my new checkbook in my hand. This did not last long, for the time came when I had to write my first check. I was standing in line at a surf shop when I realized *I was going to have to write in front of somebody.* My palms grew sweaty, and the adrenaline began to flow. It was the worst feeling in the world, and really can't be described in words. Not only was I faced with the problem of writing, but also with disclosing my inability to another person. The check was for thirty-five dollars. I pulled out one of my oldest tricks and wrote so messy that the spelling problem could not be recognized. I found out that this trick did not work with check writing when the clerk asked me to rewrite it. I got very shaky. I couldn't spell thirty, much less the name of the store. I concentrated on the things around me until I found the name of the store written on a pad nearby. To this day, I don't know if I spelled thirty-five correctly, but they took my check. I remember walking out of the store feeling invaded. I had been put on the spot and tested. Even though I managed to buy the shirt I wanted, this hurdle had caught me by surprise. I had not been prepared for it. But I would be next time.

With each hurdle I was confronted with the temptation to give up. As the laps grew in number, I questioned how many more hurdles there were and how many falls I would have to take and if the scrapes and bruises were worth the little bit of success I might have. At this time in my life I was being exposed to the things I would have to deal with the rest of my life. How could I deal with something that I knew so little about? I had always associated my writing and reading problems with school, but now I had to face the fact that these problems would never end.

After that first check-writing experience, I tried to prepare myself better for the obstacles that I now knew would come. Writing on my own without outside help became my biggest concern. Everything I wrote had always been checked over before I turned it in to my teachers. Now I was writing on my own more and more. Applying for my first job was very frustrating. Most potential employers wanted me to fill out the applications right there. I found myself giving excuses for why I needed to take the application home. Every time I went through the job searching ordeal, I got more frustrated with myself. How could I hold down any job when I couldn't even fill out the application? An even bigger question was how could I get into a college without knowing how to write?

College wasn't important to me as a means of furthering my education. In fact that was the farthest thing from my mind. College was a means of continuing my swimming. It had been a dream of mine for many years to swim on a university swim team. Since I had been going on dreams all my life, I saw no reason why I couldn't fake my way through college just as I had faked my way through my life. However, I was faced with the reality of being accepted by a university. Even though my grade point average was high enough to get into many colleges, my SAT scores were not. I was able to enter the University of Georgia through a special remedial program which provided intensive noncredit classes in reading, writing, and math. People who could successfully complete this program were allowed to enter the mainstream college classes. It did not take long to realize that faking was not going to get me into the real college classes. I was confronted with the reality that my dream was about to end.

Dr. Hyta Mederer was my remedial English teacher that first year. She was the first teacher ever who actually caught me in my lies. She confronted me about my writing. She noticed that something was different about my writing compared to her other students. I feel she knew how hard I was trying and saw that I was getting absolutely nowhere. She referred me to the university's learning disabilities clinic. I had been at the university long enough at this time to have become really attached to my teammates. I was also feeling something I had never felt before—a sense of belonging, and a small sense of accomplishment outside of swimming. I was succeeding in my math courses at this major university and was proud of myself for that accomplishment. I felt I was learning something for the first time in my life. I tried to convince myself that I had just had a poor education and that nothing was really wrong with me. I went through the Learning Disabilities Adult Clinic's two days of intensive testing not only because I wanted to stay at the university and swim, but also because I had a slight hope that I could actually overcome the academic problems that I had lived with all my life.

The testing showed that I had a cognitive processing deficit which affects my ability to understand and express oral and written language. In other words, I had a learning disability. This is a disability I am still trying to understand. I continue to have difficulty accepting the fact that I have a disability. All these years I thought I was just stupid. Giving it a complicated name and calling it a handicap only confused me at first. I felt as if the clinic were trying in a nice way to change the letters in the word STUPID to spell EXCUSE.

Even though I did not understand the clinic and who *they* were or what *they* were all about, *they* seemed to understand what I was going through. More importantly, they knew the different types of hurdles I was going to have to face to get through college. They offered advice and explanations. Having some kind of explanation for the problems I had lived with all my life helped, even though I wasn't sure I believed everything they told me.

Over the last three years I have learned to understand and accept the fact that I have unique learning abilities. I have passed college courses by using techniques based on my strengths. Rather than avoiding uncomfortable situations, such as reading in front of the class, I have learned to face them head-on. Because I have come to understand my unique abilities I am able to confide in my teachers, even though it is still uncomfortable for me to talk about myself. I try to meet my teachers before the quarter begins. I let them know that what I tell them about my learning difficulties is confidential. I emphasize to them that I would rather not be singled out as a special student although I might need some class modifications. I mention a few of my weaknesses, but I emphasize my strengths.

This is where I am today. I have grown stronger and more confident. I have more ambition. Yet, I am still scared—scared of the situations that lie ahead of me. I guess I won't ever stop being scared. As long as I face things head-on, there will always be a chance I might fail. I realize now that everyone, in every walk of life faces the chance of failing. But being in the race is better than being on the sidelines. I could fall, but if I do, I'll make sure to get up and finish.

THREE

Writing: My Worst Nightmare

My first memory of learning to write was in the second grade when we started learning to write in cursive. I know I must have struggled through learning to print because I still have trouble keeping my "b's" and "d's" and "n's" and "u's" straight. However, like many other difficult or embarrassing things in my life, I have managed to bury those memories too deep to recall. I feel that it is important to try to describe what writing is like for me because writing is one of my biggest handicaps.

It is important to remember that all learning disabilities are different and that other people with learning disabilities may have difficulty writing for entirely different reasons. My unique learning abilities affect my ability to both see and hear the letters correctly, and my language disabilities affect my ability to express my thoughts.

Thoughts of writing give me a very uneasy feeling. When I am writing, everything is uncertain. I never know if anything I'm writing is correct; stopping and starting, I am constantly trying to figure out how to form the next letter or to decide what the next letter should be. Certain words are particularly difficult. For instance, I can never spell "girl" right. I go back and forth—is it "girl" or "gril?" Neither looks right. I see everything as being jagged. The rules of punctuation and spelling have never made sense. Words never seem to be spelled the way I hear them, and they never look the same way twice.

It is difficult to explain what goes on in my head when

I am trying to write because language itself is an obstacle for me. When I am trying to spell a word, it's as if there are twenty-six letters spinning around in my head, each letter having its own box. The boxes contain sounds. The letters are trying to find their boxes by finding their sounds. I don't really see them but I feel like they're up there looking for a place to settle. Only a few of the letters in my head have dropped out of the flurry into their proper boxes. For instance, the letter "b" has come to be easier to understand then other letters; therefore, I assume I have found the box containing the sound for "b." There are times when I still have trouble forming the letter because I confuse it with "d," but the sound-symbol connection has been made. I am aware that I have found this box because without hesitation, I can name some words that start with "b." I cannot do this with many letters.

The boxes in my head are not in any kind of order. The letters are flying above the boxes searching for some sort of order. All these boxes are screaming out sounds, and I cannot pull the letters down to match the sounds. I have been trying to match these boxes with their sounds for almost twenty years. It becomes very frustrating when communication depends so much on knowing these twenty-six little letters.

When I am writing I try to match the sounds with the letters the best I can. Even if I have all the time in the world I never seem to be able to match enough letters with sounds to write a word. After concentrating so hard on trying to match the letters to the boxes, I eventually force the letters into a word. The end result is that I am never sure if I have written the word correctly. After so many years of forcing the fit, the boxes are all out of shape, making it easier to place the wrong letters within. At the same time, I have to concentrate on what the final spelling looks like so I can store it in my memory. I have to remember *my* spelling so I will know the word when I come back to it. Concentration is the key here. I am concentrating so much on just finding the correct letters and figuring out how to form the letter so that I will recognize it later, that to put my ideas into some kind of coherent order is almost impossible. I feel very lucky when I have a teacher who is organized enough to put important notes on the board during a lecture. Then I simply have to worry about transferring the letters correctly onto my paper; I worry about trying to decipher what they say another time.

I did not learn how to write until I learned how to use a computer (see Appendix 2). This sounds ironic, but in my past writing was spelling, and since I could not spell, I could not write. When I discovered a word processing system with a spelling check, I finally understood that writing involved putting thoughts and ideas into some kind of written form. Knowing that the computer would catch my spelling errors, I began to ignore my spelling. Then I began to look at writing as content. This did not happen until I was a freshman in college. Before learning to use a computer, I saw writing as a bunch of spelling words that I had to reproduce in horizontal fashion. Writing was simply a horizontal spelling test.

The computer helped me to discover that there was more to writing than just spelling. First of all, the computer was something new and different and was a relief from pencil and paper. All my life pencil and paper had been a nightmare. When I picked up a pencil and paper to write, my stomach would automatically tighten, and my nightmare would begin. The computer helped me view writing in a different way. It helped me to shed my fear of the pencil and paper. Sitting down in front of a computer was not nearly as frightening to me as sitting down with a pencil and paper. For this reason, I immediately saw the computer as a sign of hope. I had never been able to put down the right words with a pencil, but sitting at a keyboard seemed to free my mind. A pencil was like a piece of dead wood in my hands, and trying to make this stick form letters always seemed awkward and difficult. When using a keyboard, however, the letters seemed to come out through my fingertips. The writing seemed to be closer to my brain.

Not only did the computer allow me to view writing with a sense of excitement, it also allowed me to see the written symbols in a neat, organized fashion. For years I had trained my handwriting to be messy and as unreadable as possible so I could hide all my mistakes. This was a con job. When my teachers selected papers to read in class, I was sure they wouldn't read mine because they couldn't. Using a computer forced the letters out in such a neat manner that I actually started to look at the words. Before, I was afraid to look at the words. Now, instead of looking at a scribbled blurb on a page, I looked at a crisp, black-and-white image. To quote a friend of mine, it "made the words stand still." Being able to see a clear image helped me to focus on the words. I have now learned to tell when a word is wrong. I may not always be able to correct it, but the spelling check can do that for me. I have found myself trying to spell the words correctly before I put the paper through the spelling check in the word processor. Once the spelling check has checked the words, I pay attention to the change, thus reinforcing the correct spelling.

Writing in cursive is a very messy, undefined type of writing. Cursive is also an easy way out of spelling. It allows the student to compact letters together. Because of its easy flow, it does not allow the student to see how the words are actually formed. To me, it's a lazy type of writing. Before the computer, I always printed when I needed to do something right because this helped me see all the letters in the word. Even today, when I don't know a word and I don't have access to my computer, I find myself writing in cursive because it's an easy way to hide. Words I feel comfortable with, I find that I print, but words that I am not sure of, I scribble out. I believe that teachers who stress cursive writing are giving students with creative learning abilities a way out. They are allowing the student to reinforce bad habits (see Appendix 4).

Much of this chapter so far has dwelled on the subject of spelling, just as much of a person's writing education is often spent on learning to spell. If I make one point in this chapter, it is that spending so much time on trying to teach someone with a learning disability to spell might be detrimental to that person's ability to ever learn to write. I have spoken to several groups of teachers, and I am aware of how uneasy this statement makes teachers feel. However, the purpose of this book is to show what goes on in the mind of a creative learner in an attempt to explain why we have such trouble learning certain things. I cannot spell today, and it is certainly not because teachers did not try year after agonizing year to teach me. They spent so much time trying to teach me to spell that no one ever got around to teaching me how to write. To me it is an outrage that I reached college before I understood that writing is putting thoughts on paper.

For some of us spelling is impossible. Teachers and parents need to understand and accept this. It's easy for people without learning difficulties to say to the person who misspells a word to look it up in a dictionary. What they don't understand is that using a dictionary can be extremely difficult and sometimes impossible for someone who does not recognize words on paper. Distinguishing letters is extremely difficult for me. To look a word up in the dictionary takes a long time, first because I can't remember the arrangement of the letters in the word, so I have to look up different combinations until I find a word that might be close. I can often find the first two letters of a word, but the middle is always obscure. I cannot imagine what it looks like or how it sounds. When I find a word that might be close, I have no feeling about whether the word is the one I'm looking for. My feelings are more negative than anything. I'm usually more sure the word is wrong than right. An example of this is when I needed to look up the word "develop." When I first wrote this down in my notes during a psychology lecture, I spelled it "depveloup." I was so far off on the spelling that I could not begin to find it in the dictionary. This wasn't important to me because I knew what I meant the word to be and spelling has no meaning to me, but when my friends try to decipher my notes to quiz me for a test, they have no idea what language I am writing in. One thought it was French, while the other thought it surely must be Russian. My notes surely do not look as if they have been written by a good old American boy. In that same psychology class the teacher was talking about existential theory. In my notes I wrote the word as "exitenal" and "extinchail" and made a note to look it up in the dictionary later. The teacher wrote the word "existential" on the board along with some others as he was speaking. I copied all the words down without realizing that this was the same word in writing that I couldn't spell. I tried looking it up in the dictionary, but I couldn't seem to recognize it there either. I might have had my finger on it, but wasn't sure it was right. I have so much doubt about the way things are written. Sometimes teachers will spell words incorrectly on the board and the class laughs. I have no idea what they are laughing about. Interestingly, I almost get angry when the teacher misspells a word. I feel like I'm missing the show even though I have a front row seat. I guess maybe that's how some people feel when they have trouble seeing between the lines in a play or opera or when reading poetry. The frustration is similar in my case but multiplied because I am missing something that is spelled out right in front of my face.

My eye is trained not to worry about spelling. I do not misspell a word the same way each time. My spelling is not at all consistent. Every time I write a word it could be different. I am really strong with words that start with "b" and "d." I don't always put them in the right place, but I know they have a place somewhere in the word. *A, i, e, c, k, ph, f, j, o, u,* and *y* are letters that seem to give me the most trouble in spelling and reading. Notice here that all the vowels are included in this list and there are no words that do not contain vowels. Basically words that I spell right consistently are words that I have been exposed to over and over again, and they are usually short. The longer the word, the more confusing it is for me. Words that I can usually spell correctly include "the, if, was, has, were, funny, time, nice, please, people, girl, friends, Georgia, and Florida." Not many people my age can list the sum total of words they can spell with confidence within a couple lines of print!

A friend of mine who is also a creative learner told me that one of the worst years of her life was when she was in the fifth grade and her teacher made a bulletin board to encourage high spelling grades. The bulletin board was designed to look like an ocean or lake. Each student made a fish which was placed on the shore. The object was to get each fish across the ocean to the other side. This was accomplished by moving the fish according to the grade scored on the weekly spelling test. The fish could be moved a certain number of inches, depending on whether the score was 100, 90, or 80. My friend's fish never left the shore. Spelling test days were terrible for her because she had to suffer the jokes from her classmates and sometimes her teacher about how she was letting her "poor fish" die being out of the water so long. Fortunately for my friend, it was this incident that convinced her teacher that someone who participated so intelligently in class discussions but could hardly read or write had some kind of problem that needed to be investigated. She was found to have unique learning abilities and, like me, writes with the aid of a computer to correct her spelling and friends to help her proof for grammatical errors.

When every effort has been made to teach someone to spell, with no positive results, it is time to admit that the time and energy would be better spent on compensation techniques rather than on a "cure." Spelling needs to be taught as just one of the steps in writing; it should not be allowed to interfere with learning to express oneself. For me spelling was like a door that kept me from learning how to write; the computer was the key that unlocked that door. People who have a problem connecting sounds to their symbols need tools like the word processing software and the computer to help them unlock writing skills.

Language deficits

After spelling, language is the next obstacle on the way to learning to write. For people who have unique learning abilities, language skills may be limited or impaired. Language is another problem I have to face when writing. The interesting thing to me is that this is an impairment I am just learning to deal with. Spelling was always the "bad guy," but now that spelling is of less concern, I have to face the fact that I cannot always find the words I want to use, and when I can, I often cannot figure out how to string the words together to make them say what I want. The computer allows me to be inventive, to go beyond the simple words I know. For some reason, I am seldom afraid to use a word on the computer, but when I am using paper and pencil, I find myself reverting back to those old feelings of wanting to hide or to avoid putting words on paper.

Now my problem is what to do with these words that I am no longer afraid to write. What do I do when writing these words? When I am writing, I see a continuous line.

I don't see punctuation, I don't see commas, and, because I never see the punctuation, I don't stop when I read. I believe that when I was learning to read, I had so much trouble just figuring out the words that I never got around to seeing how the words are used or where the punctuation is. I could never get past the first step; actually, I hardly ever got to the end of a sentence. Like spelling, my teachers and parents could not "cure" this problem either. I still struggle so much with reading individual words that I don't see where sentences or paragraphs begin or end. I never see any structure when reading, therefore I don't know how to use it when I am writing.

My approach to punctuation is similar to that of a swimmer attempting to swim the English channel. The swimmer has several checkpoints along the way. Each checkpoint gives information on where the next point is, making the English channel a straight-across swim. If the swimmer does not stop at the checkpoints to find out where to go next, he or she would soon be lost. If the swimmer were to concentrate so much on the potential problems along the way, such as the cold or the possibility of sharks, he or she might swim right past all the checkpoints. A period is a checkpoint, and like the English channel swim, a paper has many checkpoints. Without them, the reader would become lost and confused. The paper would be one long sentence, a never-ending swim. Without the commas, the periods, the quotation marks, the reader gets lost, just like the swimmer.

Like the misguided swimmer, when writing, I would put my head down and pray that I could withstand the cold and that the sharks wouldn't get me, and I would just swim and swim and swim. Again, I feel like the computer helped me break this habit and forced me to see my thoughts in an orderly form. With the computer, I have learned to look up and see where I am headed. Just like a face mask would help a swimmer, the computer screen helps me with punctuation because it seems to make the thoughts clearer. When I write with pencil and paper, I can never see my complete thoughts. However, on the computer I can type rather quickly, and I do not concentrate so much on spelling, so I seem to type out a complete thought at once. I can see where the thought ends, and I know that some form of punctuation is needed in this pause or space. I am not always sure what goes in the space, but I know to stop, and I now have the confidence and knowledge to stop and figure out what goes there.

Paper and pencil were always my worst nightmare, whereas I see the computer as a friend. It is not judgmental. I don't have to be afraid of failing, even when confronted with my weaknesses, and the weaknesses are there. The mistakes stand out clearly in black and white. However, I can now view my errors as being correctable mistakes rather than failures, whereas with paper and pencil it is almost impossible to feel anything but failure and defeat. Using the computer seems to relieve my anxiety to the point that I can focus my attention on the organization of what I am writing.

When I was a freshman and was tested by the Learning Disabilities Adult Clinic, I was told that my language deficits affect my use and understanding of semantics and syntax in oral and written language. I have spent quite some time trying to figure out exactly what that means. The fact that I have deficits in understanding language interferes with my understanding the explanations of my problems. I can't understand the words and only through words can I understand!

Semantics pertains to the meaning of language or words, while syntax is the way in which the words are put together to form phrases and sentences. Once I came to realize that writing was more than spelling, I began to see how semantics and syntax, or word usage and sentence structure, were involved in the writing process. It was then that I gradually began to understand my language deficits and how these deficits interfered with my ability to express my thoughts in writing.

Semantics, or word usage, is really two different kinds of problems for me. One problem is thinking of the word that I really want to use, and the second is having to choose a different word because I cannot spell my first choice. Before I began to use a word processor to write, my written vocabulary was limited to words I could spell (see Appendix 2). Even though I knew there was a word that expressed exactly what I wanted to say, I would often go with an alternative, a simpler word. Even though the alternative would probably be misspelled, it would be closer to being recognized than the first choice. After doing this for many years, I simply stopped trying to use new words and just looked for words I could come close to spelling. After using the same words over and over, looking for the simplest choice has become a habit I am finding difficult to break.

I work on improving my vocabulary, but learning new words is difficult because I do not seem to be able to see them or hear them in my mind. I guess my worst problem with semantics is not being able to find the word I want to use. I know there is a word that would express exactly what I want to say; however, it is so difficult to find the exact word I want that I automatically replace the word I am searching for with an easier word. In composing a sentence, I place considerable concentration simply on semantics—finding the correct word.

Words and meanings are two different things to me. I can immediately attach meaning to some words simply because I have repeated them over and over. But most words, particularly larger words, simply disappear from my mind, even when I make an effort to retain them. The meaning may not be difficult to comprehend, but attaching the meaning to the word is extremely time consuming.

I feel like I put as much time and effort into learning English words as most Americans would have to put into learning Russian. It would not take me any more time to learn ten simple vocabulary words in Russian than it would to learn ten difficult words in English.

I am always stopped by the letters. If individual letters have no meaning, then how can they form words that have meaning? I cannot ever remember the words because I cannot see them or hear them in any consistent form in my mind. It is not the words I cannot read or write, it is the letters. When I attempt to spell a word, I try to spell the word as a whole because I cannot break the word down into individual letters. I think I might have become a better speller if teachers had focused less on teaching the letters and more on teaching syllables. It is a natural sequence for teachers to begin with teaching the sounds and symbols that make up the words of our language. Most students would learn the sound-symbol associations and proceed to apply them to the formation of words. For students who cannot comprehend the connection, another method of teaching reading and writing must be found. With me, my education ended at this point because neither I nor my teachers ever got past the letters.

I concentrate so much on learning to connect words with meanings that I lose track of the context. The problem is compounded when I am trying to scribble out a word so that I will recognize it and know the meaning of it when I look at the paper an hour later. Sometimes I am unsure of using a new word in a paper because I might not know what the word means later. Also, I use lots of words and never have a clue as to what they mean. Somehow I pick up on the feeling of the word, and I use it because it feels right in a certain context even though I do not know what it means. For example, I really don't know what the word "propaganda" means, but sometimes

I can throw it into a paper and am congratulated on how well it fits into the context of the sentence.

Once I find the words I want to use to express my thoughts, I then have to figure out the order they should go in to make sense. My poor written syntax stems from my poor oral syntax. When speaking to people my thoughts go faster than I can talk. This often happens in my writing as well. I think something and try to write it down before I forget it, and the sentence just comes out in a jumble of words that makes no sense. The lack of understanding of word definition and my poor spelling skills hold me back from writing the words as fast as I can.

Because I am not sure of the meaning of words, I often have to stop and start when trying to get out a complete thought. This results in loss of concentration. Not only do I lose what I am writing down, but I forget what I am trying to say. It's like going down a busy highway, where you're constantly having to stop at red lights or yield at yellow lights. The traffic is so stop and go that you get distracted, lose your way, and suddenly find yourself on a side street, unable to get back into the flow of traffic.

My difficulty with syntax results in sentences that are awkward. In addition to misusing words, I often leave them out. In the essay that I wrote for the Regents' Exam, I left out the main subject of the paper, the word "stool," in two sentences (see Appendix A). I have wondered if the scorers simply overlooked the errors because it was such an unusual thing for a writer to do. Sometimes I turn words or phrases around; sometimes they come out completely backwards. Sometimes the sentences are just wordy because I am trying to get back on track with my thoughts. I cannot really explain why I write like this except that I am concentrating so much on the spelling and meaning of individual words that fluency is impossible. Using the computer has helped because it makes it easier to proof my writing. Proofing is a problem in itself because I cannot see when I have left out words or reversed their order. I read the sentences as if they were correct. But now there are computer programs that will check for grammatical errors, and I also have a few friends who I trust enough to proof my papers. I have also worked on developing a style of writing that is syntactically simple, yet adequate to express the abstract ideas that are called for in college.

I have worked for four years on developing my own style of writing. It began when I was working on trying to pass the Regents' Exam. This is an exam required by the state of Georgia to prove that students are able to read and write on a college level. The exam consists of a reading section and a writing section, and a student must pass both parts before graduating. I passed it on my second try. In order to do this, I really had to work on changing my style of writing. Because of my deficits in syntax, I often wrote extremely awkward sentences that could range anywhere from a paragraph to a page in length. These sentences were usually devoid of all punctuation. If I did use punctuation, it probably did not belong where I put it. With my learning disabilities specialist, I began to work on writing short and precise sentences. At first this was very difficult because I had difficulty expressing myself and was afraid people would not understand what I was trying to say. I had a tendency to ramble on and on trying to explain myself. I was so insecure in my writing that I was very self-conscious about what other people would think of it. I had to learn to shorten my sentences, while at the same time, get across my ideas.

There was another problem in writing short sentences. College professors seem to associate intelligent ideas with long and complex sentences. I had to learn to write short sentences that would also present my ideas in an acceptable college format. I learned to do this by practicing brevity and finding descriptive adjectives that added depth to my writing. The thesaurus became one of my best friends, and other doors opened up as I learned new words. Now my papers stood out in the classroom because they were not typical of college writing, yet they delivered the depth and understanding of a college writer.

A change in attitude

If I am such a terrible writer, why am I writing this book? The truth is I have learned to love writing. I find it sad that most people with unique learning abilities hate to write. I don't find it unusual because of all the problems they have to deal with in order to write a single word on paper. I have learned to put aside my fear of writing long enough for my ideas to show through. This is part of my effort to focus my anger on fighting my disability rather than being angry with the world because I have a disability.

Writing, like anything else, has many different aspects. The important aspect of writing is the substance, not the mechanics. Writing is a form of communication, and yet many people treat it as if it is a form of punishment. Writing is beautiful. It can express the depths of a person's soul. It is a way of talking without opening the mouth. Students with learning disabilities need to experience this.

I was in college before I discovered that even though the mechanics are very important, there comes a time when a person should just let go of the mechanics and write with feeling. If teachers wait to teach the communication and aesthetic aspects of writing until their students are able to perfect the mechanics, their students may never experience the true pleasure of writing. When I let go of the mechanics and began to concentrate on what I was saying, I found that my writing improved, and in turn, my mechanics improved. Before college I hated writing because it was exposing and confronting a weakness and because it simply meant that I couldn't spell or correctly punctuate a sentence. I never once realized that writing was supposed to have meaning. As it turns out, writing is a joy.

My first insight into writing as it *should* be was in my first college English class. My teacher had us keep a weekly journal. Each week I could write about anything I wanted, and I was only supposed to take ten minutes. I was not supposed to worry about punctuation or spelling. At first this assignment scared me. I knew I would have to put more than ten minutes into it simply to get a "Pass." In fact, I typically put three hours into each journal entry.

We could bare our souls about a serious problem, describe a pretty girl walking down the street, or just describe what we had for breakfast. The point of the journals was to get us to write without being encumbered by any restraints. I found myself liking the idea of letting everything go, and even though I knew it was impossible for me to do that, I found a certain feeling of peace knowing that a grade would not be assigned to the thoughts I put on paper.

So I started to write my weekly journals. It was very hard at first. I found myself fighting to put my words on paper. I was fighting myself and the memory of years of discouragement. I did not like the fact that I had to struggle so hard and that it was so difficult to put things on paper. The freedom I longed for was not there. It was not as easy as the teacher had made it sound in class. What was supposed to be a ten-minute assignment turned out to be a week-long writing project. Then one day it happened. I was staring out the window of my dorm room and feeling sorry for myself when I saw two girls walking down the street. I had seen them around campus before.

One of them was visually impaired. She had thick glasses and carried a cane. She always seemed to be smiling. She also always seemed to be alone. Walking beside her was another girl. She was a "little person" whom I had also seen around campus, also smiling. However, she, too, always seemed to be alone. I remember passing them individually on campus and trying not to feel sorry for them. I could not help thinking about how lonely each girl must have been. I never saw them with anyone. Outside my window, walking down the chilly, lamplit street, under a starry sky, they had found each other. I realized that they were no longer alone. A warm feeling came over me, and I wanted to share it with someone.

There was no one around—only my pencil and paper. For the first time I wanted to put my thoughts down on paper. And I did. (See Appendix 3.) Forgetting about the structure, the organization, and yes, even the spelling, for the first time I was able to concentrate on the meaning. It was such a good feeling to see two people finding each other that it overrode any fear I had of writing. After I finished I realized I had written my first real paper. The paper was lousy, but I felt fantastic. Suddenly I realized the pleasure that came with putting my thoughts down in writing. For the first time I realized that, just as the blind girl had found her friend, I had found mine—writing. I was able to free my thoughts on paper. They had always been there, in my mind, but were bound by my lack of understanding of the mechanics. For the first time the mechanics were not an obstacle. Now the thoughts were free. I had never before done this. The fact that my journal was full of errors meant nothing. I turned it in just as it was, hoping the teacher would say how good it was. She never did. But it did not matter, because it meant something special to me, and it opened up a new world.

FOUR

Reading: Making the Words Come Alive

"People without hope don't write novels; but what is more to the point, they don't read them."

—Flannery O'Connor

*I*magine a little boy, happy, healthy, and energetic throughout the school day. Reading time comes: the separation of individual students placed in categories depending on their reading abilities. He becomes pale. His pace slows. His mood changes. His eyes widen as he looks toward the corner where his group (the Blackbirds) gathers. He wonders as he walks slowly past the Bluebirds and the Redbirds what it would be like to be in their groups—to be one of THEM. He knows where he belongs, however, and so does everyone else. The Blackbirds have yet to leave the nest. They wait in the corner, struggling for survival in a world where little birds (children) must be able to read in order to fly. The classification has been made. The tag has been put on, a tag that will remain throughout his school career.

His imagination flies as the group begins to read a story. As each bird struggles through the words, his imagination expands. Through his imagination, the sky opens and he soars. Nothing can stop him . . . until it becomes his turn to read. The bird falls. His imagination must be locked away as he too struggles with the words. What about this imagination? Given a chance to soar,

39

what stories could this bird tell? Imagine the vivid de-scriptions his *stories would entail. What books could he write? What philosophies could he create? What skies could he conquer? We will never know because his imagination is locked within a cage of letters.*

It was nine long years before someone released my imagination from that cage to soar one more time.

Marshall McLuhan, a well-known Canadian educator, once stated that we are all prisoners of the printed word. McLuhan theorizes that society changed with the invention of the alphabet and questions what parts of ourselves we have lost because of our reliance on the printed word. I feel like I am a prisoner of the printed word. If I lived in a society in which the printed word were not important, I would have no learning disability. In fact, in that kind of world, I might have advantages over others. Those who now communicate only through reading and writing might look up to me, a person who has untold talents in unwritten communication. It took a long time for me to realize and accept that written language is the most important aspect of learning. For many years I viewed words as my enemy. They have kept me from doing the things I want to do and from demonstrating my knowledge. Keeping me under lock and key, words have restrained me from any sense of achievement in society's view of intelligence. Students like me find themselves behind bars of words. It is imperative that teachers and parents find a way to remove the bars and set our minds free to explore our potential.

Attaching sounds to words/distinguishing words

The first step in reading is learning to discriminate letters by sound and by sight. I had trouble with both right from the beginning. My auditory deficits make it almost impossible for me to attach sounds to the individual letters of the alphabet, so my teachers had little success in teaching me the phonetic approach to reading. (They were very concerned about my difficulty, however, and insisted year after year that I have my ears checked. The one thing I was sure of as a child was that I had excellent hearing!) Nevertheless, sounding out words was never my real problem in learning to read. I seldom got to that point because I had so much difficulty distinguishing the letters in a word well enough to attempt to sound them out. My visual processing deficits seem to have interfered primarily with learning to read; these deficits continue to be an obstacle even today.

I do not have as much trouble distinguishing between individual letters, but as soon as the letters are combined, I'm in trouble. For example, I do not have trouble distinguishing between *a* and *A*; however, when the letters are combined with other letters in a word such as "as," the nature of the word seems to change so that "as" and "As" appear to me as totally different words. I can distinguish between these two words, but it would take me a few seconds longer than the average person to realize that they are the same. As words get longer, they get more and more impossible. In looking at the word "proud" in two different sentences, I have to carefully analyze the middle letters to determine that these are the same words. Reading, to me, is analyzing each word. I have to analyze carefully because sometimes my brain sticks in extra letters when I look at a word so that "proud" may look like "proud" sometimes while at other times it may look like "pround." When this happens, I think to myself, "*there is no such word as 'pround'*," and reanalyze it to come up with the more sensible "proud." If someone put the words "pound," "proud," and "pround" in a line and asked me to pick out the word "proud," I have serious doubts as to whether I could accurately perform the task because these words look the same to me.

The longer and more complex the word, the less likely I will be able to distinguish it from a similar one. I had difficulty with a recent botany question because the question began with the word "Ascomycota" and ended with "ascomycota." At first I saw these as two different words, neither of which I knew. As soon as someone read the question to me, I immediately comprehended the words and knew the answer. On that same test one sentence contained the words "genetically" and "generally," words which are different and not interchangeable. I read them as the same word, making the question impossible to comprehend. Reading is very tedious and tiresome for me because of the analysis required to distinguish words which seem to change in structure simply because they are italicized or written in bold print or capital letters.

Reading things written in cursive is almost impossible. When I was a child, I remember watching my mom write letters. I was in the second grade and just beginning to learn to write in cursive form. In watching her, I remember being very curious about this new style of writing. I could make no connection between it and the printing I had learned in first grade. It all looked like one long word to me, a word that stopped only at the end of each line. How could this word have meaning? It seemed as if it was a different language altogether. In thinking back I realize that this was the beginning of my imprisonment.

Words that have similar letters or letters that are easily reversed take a great deal of concentration to decipher even though they may be very simple words to most people. For instance, a simple word such as "top" is easily read as "pot." As a child these words were impossible for me. I remember thinking as I was walking along the sidewalk coming home from school one day that the words in my reading book were like the different sections of that sidewalk. Each sidewalk section contained a letter, and it just stretched out for miles before me—miles of letters that other people somehow turned into words that somehow connected together to make a story. I could walk up and down the sidewalk and try to find the letter combinations that made words, but by the time I found the period that signified the end of a sentence, my classmates would have traveled out of my sight.

To stay at the pace of the class, I had to learn to race though reading passages without looking at the individual words. This accounts for the confusing fact that my reading comprehension is better than my word recognition skills. Teachers have difficulty understanding how I can gain meaning from a sentence when I cannot read most of the words in that sentence. I really can't explain how I do this, but I think it came from having to find some other means of reading than going word by word. Now I tend to just look at the first part of a word rather than analyzing all of the letters in it; however, in using this technique I find myself constantly misreading words. For example I might read the words "scold" and "scheme" as the same words because I only look at their beginning letters. If I analyze words individually, I read too slowly to comprehend, but when I look at the sentence as a whole, I misinterpret it because I misread individual words. It's like I can see either the forest or the trees, but never both.

What I have learned to do is read enough words to get the idea of the sentence, and this context helps me figure out the words I don't know. Now I just glance at a word and attempt to decipher the meaning. If that word fits the context, it's ok, and if not, I go back and try another word. Glancing has become my major reading compensation strategy. Sometimes I have felt that glancing was cheating, and I know that part of the reason I glance is because I'm afraid I won't know the word. I have found a way to look for clues that help me figure out the words a little quicker than analyzing each letter in the word, but I realize this method is far from being foolproof or efficient.

Little words give me a lot of trouble because I tend to read over them in order to concentrate on the larger, more difficult words. To me, words such as "the," "and," "be," and "to" seem to be obstacles between the "real" words rather than the connectors they really are. It has taken some time, but I have come to understand that these little words are like the baton in a relay race. The baton is passed from person to person and is a major part of the race. The winner must have the baton to finish the race. When the baton gets to me, I seem to be unable to concentrate on my grip, and the little word falls to the ground and is left behind in the dust as I try to speed through to the end of the sentence. I imagine that other students who have trouble reading might also treat a sentence, a paragraph, a chapter, or a book, just like a race. Rather than reading for meaning or content, they are reading to finish as fast as they can. Somehow, they must learn to do both. My reading improved when I realized that keeping the content in mind helped me guess better at what the individual words were saying. Once a word has been determined, the next problem is obtaining its meaning.

Semantics in reading

Oliver Wendell Holmes said that "a word is the skin of a living thought." I have an appreciation and love for words that I did not have several years ago, and I think this is because I have had to struggle to own every word I know. Attaching meaning to words that are constantly changing is very difficult and interferes with learning new vocabulary words and remembering concepts. Learning new vocabulary words for a course in college is particularly difficult. I seldom learn how to pronounce the words. I learn to recognize them by picking out pieces of the word and trying to connect that with something about the word that will help me remember it. Because the words don't always look the same to me, I can't learn them by going over and over them. Sometimes when I see a common word, such as "not" or "might," it is as if I have never read that word before. People may have said the word, and when I see the word, I might know the meaning, but I often will not recognize the word itself. Since most courses introduce vocabulary words that are essential to the subject of the course and which will later appear on tests, I have to find a device to help me distinguish the words; usually that device deals with the organization of the letters in the words. Even though I would not be able to read the words aloud, I can learn to recognize the differences in the words so that I can attach meaning to them.

For example, the two words "ovary" and "ovule" look alike to me, and I could not read either one aloud, but it is very important to be able to distinguish between the two of them for a test and to know their meanings. I have learned to do this by connecting a letter with a meaning. The ovule is inside the ovary. I finally learned to remember this by thinking that the word with the *a* in it would come first because *a* is the first letter of the alphabet. I connected the idea that *a* would be first with the idea that the ovary was the larger of the two and would be on the outside of the other one. When I come to one of these words in my botany book or on a test, I first have to stare at the two words and try to distinguish the differences in the way they look. It is like staring at a pair of identical twins and trying to find one thing that's different enough to help you tell them apart next time. Once I find that one different detail, the next step is to employ my trick for remembering their meanings. For these two words, I try to distinguish them enough to see which has the a and which has the u. Then I can go to my trick of remembering which letter signifies which meaning. You can imagine why it takes me so long to take a test. I not only have to figure out a way to distinguish words, I also must figure out ways to remember their meanings. Try calling up a bunch of letters (like "bjros") and obtaining meaning from them. It is extremely difficult.

To me a word on a page is separate from its meaning. For example, the word "Venezuela" written on a page is not the same as "Venezuela" when I hear it spoken or see it on a map. I have no experience with Venezuela in the printed form; it has no meaning for me, and I would not recognize the word. When it is spoken, Venezuela comes to me as a picture of a country, as people, as a culture, as a news topic. It is alive and has meaning. When I am asked to locate Venezuela on a map, it is the V word in South America that I learned one time in geography class. Its meaning goes little beyond that. Words come alive for me when they make pictures in my mind. The spoken word "Venezuela" brings the picture of a country and its people to my mind. Just because I can't read a word does not mean I don't know a lot about it. Students with reading deficits are often being tested on only half of what they know. I have performed poorly on tests covering subjects that I knew all about simply because I could not read or attach meaning to the words on a test. In these cases the teachers never tested my true knowledge of the subject. It is very frustrating to have people believe you are dumb when you know that if they would just ask the question in another way, you would be able to give them all the information they'd want to know.

I do not attach meanings or draw connections as I

read; reading is simply figuring out the word that each group of letters stands for. If it is difficult to connect the letters to make words, imagine how difficult it is to connect the words to make meaningful sentences. When I can read all the words in a sentence, I still struggle to gain meaning from the sentence because I am not in the habit of reading for meaning. Even though my reading recognition has improved, I still have a tendency to try to read the words without focusing on the meaning. Once I get the words, then I try to figure out the meaning of the sentence. For most people in college, meaning comes with reading the words, but it seems as if every other sentence has a word I don't understand. Reading without meaning is like buying a carton of milk and getting only the carton. The carton is useless without the milk and the milk cannot be contained without the carton. You have to understand the words to comprehend the meaning, and you've got to have the meaning to understand the word. Understanding this connection has improved my reading comprehension, although I have had to develop my own comprehension techniques.

Part of improving my reading came with learning to trust my instincts and my intuition. When I am filled with doubt, my reading is usually poor, but when I simply race along and trust that I am getting the gist of the meaning of a passage I usually comprehend much better. I have found that I can read lots of words and never have a clue as to their actual definitions, but somehow I pick up on the *feeling* of the word. The meaning of a passage often comes to me as a feeling or picture in my mind, but seldom as words. I implicitly seem to understand things, and attempting to attach meanings to words only confuses the content for me. I have learned that if I concentrate so much on connecting words with meaning when I read, I lose track of the meaning of the entire content.

A continuing challenge

It makes sense that I often find reading to be unpleasant because it has brought little but embarrassment and anxiety. Reading is one of the most frightening things I ever had to learn in school. Students who have trouble reading not only have to struggle to decipher a bunch of squiggles on a piece of paper, they also have to face the daily fear of being called on to read in class. Many people don't like to read in class because they are shy, but students with reading difficulties agonize over reading aloud because they know they will be embarrassed in front of their friends. This is why many students rebel. The one time I was asked to read in class was in the seventh grade. I was called on to read a sentence on the blackboard, and was so terrified that I blacked out. I could not say a word when Sister Anne called on me. Thinking that I was being defiant, she told me to go to her office after class. I admitted to her that I had blacked out, but not that I couldn't read the sentence. She called my mom because she was concerned about my health, but she never probed further and never seemed to realize that I could not read a word that was on the board. When confronted by Sister Anne in her office, I denied to her and to myself that the real problem was that I couldn't read. This was a natural reaction. I did not want to face the fact that I was stupid. I was training my mind at an early age to shut out my problem and automatically concoct a legitimate way out.

As a child, my impression of words was that they were black and white, very dull, colorless, and boring. Things have changed. Now I see those same words as a key to freedom. This came from listening to teachers explain what the written words mean. I was in my second year of college before the breakthrough came. I was allowed freedom. I was allowed to read and explore different views. I would struggle to read my assignments the night before and then the teachers would make them come alive through class discussion. I found myself actually listening and being motivated to participate, or if not participate, at least explore my own opinions for myself. I realize that we must have discussed books in my high school classes, and I am not quite sure how those discussions were different and why they weren't as meaningful as the ones I had in college. I really don't remember things ever coming alive for me when I was in high school.

When I look back on my high school English classes, I really can't remember much creativity at all. It seemed that everything was always focused on grammar. The high school teachers seemed to emphasize the basics of English, and we forgot all about the enjoyment and creativity that comes from reading great literature. It was as if we left the stilted reading groups of elementary school behind and never read for pleasure again. Literature was touched on in high school, but far less than it should have been. I think that high school should be a time for exploring and examining different thoughts and ideas through literature, but the emphasis in my school seemed to be on passing basic competency tests. All possible joy in learning was lost. I feel that if we can't grasp basic grammar before entering high school, we should have two separate classes—one for literature and one for grammar—and maybe even another one for writing. Students like me, who had difficulty learning grammar, are doomed to study grammar every year. We are good thinkers, but are never given the opportunity because we are bogged down in the impossible (for us) quest to comprehend grammar. Teachers should take the opportunity to expose students to the ideas of others through literature and teach them to think and express their opinions, opinions that are valued as important. A class such as this might possibly compensate for the negative feedback we receive from years and years of trying to learn the impossible rules of spelling and grammar. Teachers must realize that English does not mean just grammar and spelling and that students who are required to master those rules are not being allowed to taste the pleasures of literary writing. It is possible to appreciate the written words of literature without understanding the grammar involved.

Teachers argue with me that they cannot teach literature to students who cannot read. If my teachers and I believed that, I would not be writing this book. Educators need to realize that if a student has trouble reading, it is their responsibility to get the student involved. The best way to do this is to read to them and with them, making the words come alive. Students with learning difficulties have to be encouraged more than the average student because they are afraid of failure, afraid they might be embarrassed in front of their peers, just plain afraid of the words. The teacher can prevent this by demonstrating for the class how to read literature.

A friend of mine told me about how one of her teachers singlehandedly changed her negative attitude about reading. This seventh grade teacher read to her class for an hour every afternoon from books written to appeal to the young and adult reader. The class didn't always understand every word, but the teacher would stop and talk about new words and talk about the plot and ask them for their opinions from time to time. For Christmas, this teacher gave each child a copy of the book, *The Secret Garden*. She told the class to bring their books back to school after the Christmas break. The teacher started off the new year by reading this book again to the class during reading hour. Only this time, the whole class had their own books to follow along with her as she read. She would stop from time to time and let them fill in words and ask them what they thought about the book to that point. On their own people began reading ahead to find out what would happen. My friend had never enjoyed reading before, but she kept reading ahead and finished the book long before the teacher did. She said it was one of her greatest pleasures to carry that book around with her knowing she had read the entire book and could discuss it with anybody who cared to know what she thought. The words had come alive for her, and without realizing it she had also learned some reading techniques that helped her tackle other books on her own.

The words came alive for me for the first time in Amelia Davis Horne's English 101 class. I will never forget the experience. The room had the frigid atmosphere of a typical English class until she walked in. Her eyes radiated excitement. Coming from her mouth were words of substance, of meaning, of poetry, of understanding. Descriptions of the course structure seemed trivial compared to the way she described the adventure on which we were about to embark, through literature. She spoke with exhilaration, and the topics provoked vivid pictures in our minds. Curiosity vibrated within us; literature came alive.

Keys to unlock the prison door

At the beginning of this chapter, I mentioned that I often feel like a prisoner of the printed word. I envision myself locked in a circular prison in the middle of a dark room with only one piercing light to leave a separate shadow . . . a shadow of struggle. I am trying to escape the bars, to slip through the prison of words. My eyes focus. I can see words surrounding the gray scope in front of the cage, but they only disappear into the dark lost realm of sentences—a place full of stories and facts, newsletters, newspapers, textbooks, novels, and poetry—all escaping my reach. I am not allowed to partake of their knowledge. I am not allowed to grow. All my ideas and thoughts are imprisoned with me. There can be no freedom. I reach again, only to miss the word that was once in sight. If only the light would focus away from the cage and out into the gray boundaries. The few words I can read form images in my mind. My mind is open, but another word goes by, beyond my grasp. The word isn't clear enough for me to distinguish. I call on my shadow to reach out as far as it can go to try to see this word and relay it to me, but sometimes it can't. My shadow enables me to see a few of the words . . . a line of poetry, a morsel of knowledge. Grabbing hungrily at the morsel, I throw it together with the other pieces, slowly filling the cage. This feels good. I may not be able to escape, but I can bring the knowledge into my cell. I hunger for more information, but the little morsels keep me going.

However, sometimes my shadow relays the wrong message. It brings back a word, but it isn't right. It brings back a word so similar that I don't realize it is not the word I needed. It's a trick. Sometimes I make myself believe it's the right word and quickly throw it on the cell floor. I am angry when I find out from a passing guard that the word is wrong. I chastise myself. Why can't I be like that guard—free to go out and gather the words as I need them rather than simply waiting for them to come within my reach? What can I do to get out of this cage? To see those words? To experience the total freedom?

As with any creative learner, I have had to create my own system; I have had to find my own keys. Although the keys are not conventional, they allow me to unlock my cell and escape for awhile. One of the most useful keys I have discovered is one that is available to anyone with a reading disability—recorded books. Although I began by simply getting my textbooks on tape, I explored further and found that printed books of all kinds were available on tape. *The key to reading was listening . . . listening to the author's words communicated to me by some other reader.*

Talking Books are available through Recordings for

the Blind, a federally established program to provide textbooks and other written materials to people who are visually impaired or have reading disabilities. It costs a small fee to apply, and the application must be accompanied by documentation from a teacher or psychologist verifying that the student has a reading disability. The student is assigned a number and given a list of available reading materials. The list is constantly updated, so many books may be available even if they are not listed. Instructions are provided as to how to order materials, and the material is free to those who qualify, along with a special tape recorder that is necessary to listen to the four-track tapes.

Getting my textbooks on tape was one of my major tools in college, although it took some time to learn to use them properly. Because I had spent so much time struggling with words, I had missed out on learning the comprehension skills necessary to gain understanding from the material. I found that I had as much difficulty simply listening to the tapes as I had in trying to read the book. I eventually learned that following along in the text while listening to the tape was the best method for me. After using this technique for a few months, I was pleasantly surprised to discover that my general reading ability (without tapes) was improving. I believe the tapes helped me find a reading rhythm I had never had before, and I know they improved my word recognition skills. Just as the computer helped me learn to distinguish letters as I typed them in, the tapes helped me learn to distinguish individual words. As I saw and heard a word, such as "that," repeated over and over in a text, I found that I began to recognize it before the tape recorder said it. My reading today is smoother and more comprehendible because I learned what good reading should be from listening to tapes as I read along in the text.

Just as many teachers object to students using a spelling check computer program rather than learning to spell, many will resist obtaining textbooks on tape for students because they view it as a crutch. Taped texts are not a crutch, but a key to unlocking a world of words that has been denied to some of us with unique learning abilities. These students have the intelligence to understand written material, but lack the tools to get to the information. Taped texts simply allow access, and students must be taught how to use (read) them just as they are taught to read and comprehend books. I do not use taped texts for all of my courses, but I have found that they are particularly helpful with the voluminous reading material that comes with literature classes. I have also started buying my own books on tape. Now when everyone is discussing Tom Clancy's *Hunt For Red October*, I can join in the discussion—not because I have seen the movie, but because I have read (listened to) the book.

Taped texts only solve part of the problem of having to struggle to read. Most written material is not available on tape. We are constantly bombarded with the written word—on tests, on the blackboard, on notes from friends and parents, on TV, and on the highway. Copying words that I can't read helps. When I come to a word I do not know, I first try to sound it out. If I can't come up with a word that makes sense in the context of the sentence, I copy the word on a piece of paper. This forces me to write down each letter. It is very possible that my brain was missing a letter or two. I find that it helps me to separate the letters and get to know them (*Hello* B. *My name is Chris. What is* your *name*?). If I am lucky, it will say its name slowly enough for me to understand, and then I can place it back in the word and begin again.

Another key is to slow down. All my life, I have never been able to read well, so I am always going through material very quickly. I have found that when I slow down, I read the words better. One of the problems with this is that in slowing down, I often find myself forgetting the content of the passage. I can deal with this by reading the passage twice—once for words and once for content. For long passages this is not a good key to use, but for shorter ones, it works just fine.

The complicated textbooks that come with college course work present me with a real challenge because reading each chapter twice is simply not possible. I had to develop my own technique, which I call the "Christopher Lee Backwards-Forwards (B-F) Reading Technique." (Many people call this "previewing and reviewing," but they are not creative learners.) There are two ways which I can choose to attack a chapter. I can do a preview outline, or if I don't have the time, I simply go ahead and read; however, I never read every word in the chapter. Because I have trouble deciphering words I have a tendency to lose focus of the content throughout the chapter. As the chapter progresses I lose the connection between the beginning and end. When time permits I make an outline of the chapter before I start studying so that I can find that link *before* I start reading. I can then keep this link in mind as I read. This helps but is only the beginning. In previewing a chapter in my psychology book, for example, I start an outline based on the subheadings in the chapter:

Psychological Theories of Adjustment
    I. Psychodynamic Theory
        A. Sigmund Freud: Id, Ego, and Superego
        B. Modern Psychodynamic Theory
            1. Erich Fromm (Personality & society)
            2. Erik Erikson (development in a social context)
    II. Behavioral Theory
        A. Walter Mischel: The Interaction of person and situation
            1. Cognitive behaviorism

III. Humanistic Theory
   A. Abraham Maslow: The Hierarchy of Needs
   B. Carl Rogers: The self theory
IV. Existential Theory
   A. Viktor Frankl

As I make the outline, my concentration is on writing. Each word I copy down appears to be different, even when they are the same. For instance, when I wrote "Modern Psychodynamic Theory," I did not realize at the time that it included the same words I had written down in #I. I have to concentrate so much on reading and writing when I am making the preview outline that I really don't *comprehend* the material. This is when I use my B-F Technique. **I write Backwards. I read Forward.** This is easier than it sounds, though confusing to explain.

In outlining, I write down the organization of the chapters by picking out the key concepts that are written in bold or italicized print, including titles, subtitles, and vocabulary terms. As I write, I continuously go *backwards* over what I have already written to see if anything matches since I don't always recognize the words. For example, when I write the words "Existential Theory" (IV), I follow my pencil back up the Roman numerals to see if I've written this word or anything linked to it before. If I can't find anything, I continue forward. This is what I call *writing backwards*. I continuously review what I've written to maintain the links between each highlighted idea.

If I choose not to outline a chapter first, it's very important that I read ahead to be able to see which words repeat themselves in the chapter. If I'm reading a chapter and come to a new word or concept, then I look ahead to see if it's mentioned again in any of the subtitles or writing under pictures or in italicized or bold print. As writing backward does, *reading forward* helps me make the links throughout so that the whole chapter is tied together. It is easy to read a chapter or skim over it; the hard part is knowing what it says. At times I bog down in deciphering the words and forget that the purpose of reading is to obtain information. The B-F Technique always helps me keep the content in mind. Writing an outline and checking backwards (reviewing) what I have written keeps me tuned in to new vocabulary words that are repeated often but that I might not recognize. Reading forward (previewing) to see if this word is mentioned in the rest of the chapter helps me learn to recognize the word as well as learn its meaning. This method was time consuming when I first started using it, but after awhile it became second nature and I now find it much more efficient than attempting to read every word in the chapter. I have learned how to draw information from chapters without having to spend all week reading that one chapter.

Reading is not pleasurable; it is work, and for me it is frustrating. Reading relates to school, and if your self-confidence is low in school, there is a chance you will never have an incentive to read. I find myself enjoying listening to books rather than reading them, but I think it is important to read something every day to build your skills. Through the tapes I have learned how to enjoy the stories, and this new pleasure has made me want to strengthen my reading skills.

Unlock your prison

Here is the most important point: Don't let yourself be imprisoned in a cage. Reading can be a prison if you let it. A prison is a cold and lonely place with very few stories told and not too many questions answered. It's a place where people can become narrow-minded, not expanding their ideas and horizons. Books are valuable sources of information. They give us ideas and tell us stories and teach us history through words. Books are a way of communicating. Don't let yourself be limited to one form of communication. The written word is as important as the spoken word, and no one knows that better than me. I almost locked myself into a prison—a prison of no words, no mystery, no adventure, no growth, no flying, no freedom. I was imprisoned—until I discovered the experiences held within words.

FIVE

Language: Making It Real

My strongest memories come from the second grade . . .

A lady with soft blond hair pulled back into a loose bun . . . jewelry, embracing her wrist, guides her hand as a gesture flows through the air . . . a fragrance, sweet and scintillating, echoes around her as she moves through the room . . . a voice, soft and comforting, is punctuated with concern.

A room . . . thickened with paint . . . bare of designs . . . basically empty . . . A chair and table in the middle topped with black folders, flash cards, and game boxes, all designed to fix me.

A small boy . . . eyes fixed on the big black boxes on the table . . . glancing up to view the jewelry . . . interesting and exotic . . . back to the boxes. Is this the answer? Can these boxes fix me? Is this lady the angel I asked for? Can the charms on her jewelry work magic and make me talk like everyone else?

Verbal communication

My parents became concerned about my speech and language ability when I was three years old and had not begun to talk. They took me to a specialist who thought at first that I might just be slow in developing but later told my mom that my problems seemed to be more than developmental or simple articulation. Basically my speech disability was the first sign that something deeper was wrong; however, it was many years before another diagnosis was made. I had not made much progress in language development by the time I reached school, but the school had the answer. They suggested I had a simple articulation problem that could easily be fixed by a speech teacher. I was placed in speech classes almost immediately, the first of many times that I would be separated from my friends to attend a "special" class. When I think back on it, it would have been nice if all I had had was a simple speech problem that could have been cured with a few hours of speech lessons each week.

Looking back, I find it interesting that during all of the time I spent with the speech teacher, the only concern seemed to be over how I was placing my tongue and how I was pronouncing my words. It never occurred to anyone that I might have a language disability. I know a lot of students who went through speech classes because they could not say certain letters or words correctly. They would learn to correct their articulation problems, leave the class, and move on to success. My articulation problem appeared to be more difficult to cure. I simply could not pronounce things the right way, and it seemed that it might be because I was not hearing things the right way. I have had many hearing tests over the years and some people still think that the reason I speak the way I do is because my hearing is poor. I know now, however, that the problem is not with the way I hear words but with the way my brain *processes* what I hear. My speech teachers spent many years concentrating on my expression when the problem was actually my reception.

I have learned to speak based on how my brain interprets what I hear. This is considered to be an auditory processing disability. The sounds we use for speech change depending on the combinations of consonants and vowels. I have trouble with *r*'s and *l*'s, particularly when they are combined with vowels. When I put *r*'s and *l*'s with vowels, the vowel sound becomes different so that I cannot distinguish those vowel sounds from each other.

This discrimination problem hinders me not only in understanding what a word is, but also in picturing the word in my mind. I tend to rely heavily on forming images in my mind to get meaning from words, but if I cannot understand the word, the image is blurred. For example, the word "purpose" has always been a blur to me because the combination of "ur" gives me such trouble. To this day I cannot begin to look this word up in a dictionary because I cannot imagine how it would be spelled. I pronounce the middle of this word as I do the word "book" so I would first imagine that it is spelled "poopus." I have learned that the *oo* sound can be made by a *u*, so I might also try to look the word up as if it were spelled "poupus." It would never occur to me that the word has an *r* in it because *r*'s seem to be nonexistent in my language system.

The fact that I "see" sounds is usually very interesting to the specialists who have worked with me. I was not aware until recently that other people do not typically do this. I have mentioned that words written in cursive are much harder for me to read than words written in printed form. Similarly, I write (compose) and spell more accurately when using a word processor because the letters appear before me in a much clearer, crisper manner than words I write in cursive. The way I hear (see) sounds is similar to the difference between reading and writing printed and cursive letters. When sounds are spoken clearly and crisply in a straightforward manner, I picture them in my mind as being printed letters or letter combinations. When people speak rapidly or in different tones of voice, the sounds come into my mind written in cursive, making them difficult to distinguish.

Probably because the sounds themselves are so difficult for me to process, I gather more information from the *way* someone says the sound. In other words, I tune more into the intonation used than the actual words being said. Some intonations appear to me in print while others appear in cursive. For example, singsong voices are very difficult for me to decipher because both the intonation and the rhythm are different from average, everyday speech tones. If a person asks me if I can distinguish the two sounds, *i* and *e*, when used in isolation, I would have to say it depends on the intonation that person uses in pronouncing those sounds. If they say the letters to me in a clear, straightforward manner, I would see a printed *e* and *i* in my mind and would be able to distinguish them as two different sounds; however, if this person changed his or her rhythm and intonation into a singsong manner, I would see a cursive *e* and *i*, two letters which look (sound) alike to me.

Although most of my articulation difficulties are because I cannot distinguish certain sounds, there are some words I have trouble articulating because I cannot get the sequence of the sounds to come out in the right order. Words such as "specific" and "stethoscope" require rapid-fire sequencing. Many people trip over these words, but they are impossible for me to say, even when I concentrate. I often seem to have trouble hearing the middle parts of words, so that in pronouncing a word, I sometimes miss the middle piece of the sequence. I usually hear word endings, so plurals, possessives, and tenses have not been major problems; however, the middle of words, and sometimes the beginnings, often seem to be distorted so that all the words in a sentence might run together or sound alike. If I do not concentrate on speaking clearly, I tend to sound like I am mumbling because I run all the syllables together in a sentence; this is how they sound to me. There are certain words I have never been able to pronounce without great effort, and if these are common, everyday words, I have had to come up with some way to fake my way around them. "Stethoscope," for instance, is a word I can easily avoid, but "breakfast" is one I have always been teased about. The closest I can come is "brefix," so I just refer to this as a morning meal or "early morning food." People usually just think I'm being clever, or silly, depending on the mood of the conversation. Over the years people have always told me that I talk differently, but not unpleasantly, and some people have said they like the way I talk. However, I still feel uncomfortable with the way I pronounce my words. The lessons that my speech teacher so carefully designed to cure me never worked. Only recently have I come to understand why.

Essentially, all of the vowels sound alike to me. Only when I really concentrate and am in a one-on-one situation can I distinguish the different sounds. With lots of concentration and practice, I could reproduce the words the speech teacher would say to me in her classroom. As soon as I left there, the sounds all became muddled again. It was the speech teacher's frustration that finally led to my being removed from her class after three years. She told my mother that she didn't know what my problem was, but that it wasn't speech. It wasn't until I was tested for the learning disabilities program in college that I began to get a clear understanding that my speech problems were related to my learning problems. The fact that I could not distinguish sounds well enough to reproduce them not only interfered with my pronunciation of words, but also with the basic skills necessary for reading and writing.

In speech class, we would start by going over the assignments I was supposed to have been practicing at home. In reality I didn't practice much at home. I did not understand what my teachers wanted me to do. I did not see (hear) that I had a problem and didn't understand why I was in that class or why I had to practice those stupid lip exercises. That's all they were to me—tongue and lip exercises—because I couldn't hear any differences in sounds. I was saying what I was hearing, but I didn't know that what I was hearing wasn't the same thing that everybody else was hearing.

I imagine that what I was experiencing at this time was similar to what a colorblind child experiences. The child would know that there were such things as different colors because, just as sounds of letters are taught early, so are colors. However, a child who sees everything in black, white, and gray, would not recognize the difference among crayons of red, green, or purple. I could not hear the difference between *a, e,* and *i,* and to this day, I pronounce the words "pool," "pull," and "pearl" just alike. (Being a swimmer, it has been interesting to have difficulty with the word "pool," but I have learned to always precede it with "swimming," which allows the listener to fill in any difficulty in understanding the words "swimming pool.")

Back to speech class. I guess because of the severity of my language disability, I was placed in a speech class by myself. All I had to concentrate on was my speech teacher. I remember spending hours and hours just looking at her mouth. I think I knew every crevice of her lips and every form those lips could be molded into. We practiced rolling the tongue. To this day I am an expert tongue-roller, but I still cannot say my *r*'s correctly. Our sessions would go something like this:

> "Christopher, place the tip of your tongue on the roof of your mouth and roll it up. Repeat after me: RABBIT."
> "WABBIT."
> "No Christopher, say RABBIT."
> "RABBIT" Hurray! I would usually get it right the second time. Free candy!!
> "Say it again."
> "WABBIT."
> "No, say RABBIT."
> "RABBIT."
> "Good, Christopher."

How could she say this was good? What was going on here was that I could repeat the word "rabbit" correctly only after hearing and watching her say it. When she said to say it again, I couldn't say it. Basically all I was doing was repeating a word correctly that she had just said to me. I would get an M & M every time I said it correctly and lose the M & M every time I said it wrong, so at the end of the session I would usually end up with only the smell of M & Ms to remind me of my hard work. Occasionally, with pure luck, I surprised us both and got a couple of words right in a row. I quickly gobbled up the M & M before her hand, weighted down by jewelry, could smash down and take it away again, smearing the table with chocolate. I swear that my speech teacher had the same large bags of M & Ms at the end of the year as she did at the beginning. In fact, it came to a point at the end of the year that I didn't want to say the word right because I would have to eat one of those year-old M & Ms.

The fact is that I still cannot say my r's. When I say "girl" people think I am saying "gull." This can be very confusing to listeners since these two words are seldom interchangeable in sentences. There are other sounds that I say strangely, but the r sound is the one that causes the most heads to turn among my southern relatives and friends. Being from the South, I have always heard friendly (and not so friendly) jokes about the North, particularly about the way northerners talk. Northerners have been my salvation, however, because they have provided me with an explanation for the way I speak. I speak very fast, and I have been told that the way I pronounce my r's is similar to the way Bostonians pronounce theirs. I heard this comparison so much as a child that I remember wondering many times what it would be like to live in Boston. I thought it would be nice to live in a place where I was not the different one. I wondered if the people there had problems spelling too.

When I was younger, this difference in speaking was aggravating. However, now I have learned to use it as a way of meeting people. I find that people are very interested in where I am from because I speak so differently from others in the South. I have learned to use my language problem as an advantage, but only after finding a good way of faking it. I suspected that if I tried to explain to the people I meet that I had a speech problem it would influence their perception of me. Some people would feel sorry for me; others would feel that I am less competent than I really am and would put less trust in me. Therefore, I have engineered a system that allows me the chance to express myself without causing negative perceptions on the part of others. I fake it and tell them I'm from Boston or Providence or New York or some believable Northern city or town. This allows me to step into a relationship without tripping. I know that first impressions are important, and I am not willing to risk my intelligence on someone else's negative prejudgments.

It is interesting how faking it usually comes back to haunt me. I discovered that when someone asks me where I am from, it is not uncommon that they have been exposed to the North and are curious to know if I am from someplace they are familiar with. I have run into people who are from Boston and want to know what part of the city I am from and when I moved to the South. I would suddenly find myself in a long and twisting conversation in which I was lying (faking) throughout. I have learned that one lie provokes another, so over the years I have revised my story so that it is more believable. The story goes something like this . . .

"My dad is originally from Boston. I actually grew up in Florida; however, being around him and visiting relatives, I have picked up his accent. It's funny; my brother has done the same thing, but my sister did not pick it up." (This adds credibility to my story, and it is true that my brother has the same type of language problem that I have.)

I do not like lying, and I only use this story when I have to. I usually use this scenario in circumstances when I am insecure and need to present myself well, and it is usually used on people I know I won't see again. For instance, being a communication major, I often found myself having to speak in front of classes. The initial contact with the class was always the same: an introduction and a "condensed portfolio of our lives." (YUCK! That's right! A "portfolio of our lives"!)

> Where do I start? "My name is Christopher Lee; I'm a senior communications major from Jacksonville, Florida." (Oh, no! A raised hand already. . . . let me guess . . .)
> "Excuse me, excuse me. Are you originally from Florida?"
> "Yes, however, my father is from Boston. . . ."
> The story flows naturally from that chapter in my mind labeled "Faking It."

This story has served its purpose. It has allowed me to come into new situations on the same level with everybody else. I am accepted as a student—not a student with learning disabilities or a speech impediment. Just a student. Members of the human race tend to be superficial. It has its good points and its bad. One of its bad points is that people tend not to associate with others who are different from themselves in some way. People who don't fit the norm are more likely to be pushed aside than included in the group. If I were honest about my problems at the beginning of class, I most likely would find the majority of students shoving me away rather than including me in the group. Because my disability is hidden, I can devise a system to hide the truth. This story gets them off my back and allows me to start the class on even ground with everyone else.

We could view new situations, such as new classes, as staircases. Everybody starts off at floor level. The first step everybody has to make is the introduction—that "condensed portfolio" (YUCK!) of their lives. If I were to take that first step by saying "Yes, I've always lived in Florida; I just have a language disability," automatically, that first step would be pulled out from under me. Images would be constructed in the other students' minds. Even the teacher might create an image of me as being different from others. I might as well be in that class by myself with the teacher all to myself. But see, I'm too smart. I have learned that the best way to handle this situation is to promote a misrepresentation of my life to enable me to take that first step so that I might reach the top of the staircase with everyone else. After I have climbed each step and reached the top and felt accepted and secure, then my magic starts. I use my disability to work for me. I make them accept the disability—not only accept it, but admire me even more for achieving what I have despite the disability. This is a slow process, but it works. Approaching the problem in this manner enables me to meet face to face with each student in the class to explain my unique learning abilities to them one on one after they have accepted me for who I really am. I try to help them understand my deficits, to feel what it is like to be different, to better understand the learning disabilities community. And my classmates have friends, and those friends have friends, and yes, slowly, my "faking it" story has worked its magic, and people have a better understanding of what students with learning disabilities can really do. Then, the next time a student with learning difficulties is standing up in front of a class giving a "condensed portfolio of his or her life," one of my pupils will sit back and understand rather than prejudge unfavorably.

I have come to understand that the way I pronounce

my words is only a small part of language. Basically I have my own language system, and it is not like anyone else's. However, because I am the different one, I have had to learn to adapt to the standard communication system most people use. My analogy is that language is a mixing bowl full of ingredients. The basic ingredients are the foundation of my language. In language these ingredients are words. They come in a variety of sounds, lengths, and meanings that add richness and texture to the final concoction. In order to produce the perfect cake with the best flavor, the ingredients must be correctly proportioned and added in the right order.

This is where my problem lies. Sometimes the recipe is incorrect, and other times an ingredient is missing or not immediately available. I often have difficulty finding a word I want to say. I have learned that this is a word retrieval problem and is a part of language called semantics. Semantics is a problem for me both receptively and expressively. This is difficult to understand, much less explain, but it is most easily understood through the analogy of making a cake. So put on your chef's hat and join me in the kitchen. We start with a recipe. Recipes are written in standard formats. The ingredients are listed at the top and the directions for mixing and cooking are at the bottom. Receptive language is the list of ingredients at the top of the page. It is what goes into the cake. It is the information that goes into your brain from words that other people say to you. Expressive language is what should come out. It is a picture of the final confection or the cake itself. It is the language that you verbalize, the thoughts you express through words. If you can't find the ingredients (words) you need to use, your final product (sentence) will be lacking richness and texture (fluidity and clarity).

As I speak I am often plagued with a loss of words. I sometimes search for words to the point where I lose track of what I am saying. This retrieval problem was explained to me by Dr. Noël Gregg, the Director of UGA's Learning Disabilities Adult Clinic. She explained the mystery of word retrieval as a filing system. Some people's filing cabinets are well-organized with all of the drawers and folders neatly labeled and in alphabetical order. Other people have filing systems that are less organized and less efficient. It is easier for me to relate this retrieval concept to my immaculate "neat-freak" roommate, Lester, and my sister, Michelle. Lester, tall and clean-cut, is a large-sized poster of perfection. He takes extra time to prepare himself for the outside world. Michelle, on the other hand, is energetic and carefree. Michelle confronts each day ready for adventure, throwing perfection to the wind. Her room is an adventure in itself with clothes and shoes flung to all corners. Much of the thirty minutes she allows for dressing each morning is spent on searching for the perfect costume of the day. Lester's room, however, is like a hospital room. Scrubbed clean, the room reflects his strong sense of perfection and organization. Michelle might be described as a hurricane, leaving her mark wherever she goes, whereas Lester is the eye of the hurricane, presenting a sense of calmness and stability. Their organizational abilities are reflected in their rooms. If I were to ask Lester if I could borrow a particular shirt, he would be able to immediately go to his closet and pull out the requested shirt, neatly washed and pressed. On the other hand, if I were to ask Michelle for the shirt she had borrowed from me the week before to use in her weekly aerobics adventure, a puzzled look would cross her face. The adventure would change to a search, which would entail a little more time and thought. The shirt would eventually be found, but it might take a search team to find it.

When I am searching for a word, it is as if I am searching for a borrowed shirt from Michelle's room. I know the shirt (word) is there, but my brain cannot seem to grasp it. All people have trouble from time to time calling up the words they need. I often hear people joking about the "tip of the tongue syndrome." This is no joke to me. The disorganized filing cabinet in my brain causes me to lose entire thoughts and subjects while I am searching for one heading. It affects me not only when I am speaking, but also when I am listening. I often seem to get behind when listening to others because I misunderstand or don't know the meanings of key words. My vocabulary words are not stored in a manner that I can grasp immediately, so I am always having to search for meaning. Over the last few years I have learned that words are usually put together in a certain way so that there is a root that helps locate the heading it should be filed under. I never knew this before so I had no clue as to how to file a word away in my memory so that I could recall it later. I would learn a new word and hear it the next day and not know that I had ever heard it before. It is like having one shoe in a closet—eventually you throw it out because it's useless. I have learned now to tear new words apart to see where the word comes from, making them easier to store. The meanings are not always clear at first, but at least I am building a system where there was once only chaos.

Sometimes I have trouble pulling up words because I am not sure of the way the sentence should be structured. This is called a syntax problem. Individuals with language problems often skip over small words, such as "or," "an," and "the" because they are concentrating on getting the major words in the sentence, or the gestalt, a feeling for the sentence as a whole. In my language system these words are not important, so I skip over them. I have learned to do this as a survival strategy, not realizing that I was leaving out the words in a sentence (key ingredients) that give structure and meaning to the sentence.

It is not logical to me to try to grab every word of a

sentence when I am listening to someone speak. Instead I summarize the meaning of the sentence in my mind. I try to get the meaning of the sentence and not worry about the word order. The problem with my receptive language is that when listening to someone speak, I may omit words, reverse words, or add words to that sentence in my mind, distorting the message the speaker is trying to send. I believe that I catch only sixty to seventy percent of what people say to me. I have learned to get the gestalt, or the whole thought, by picking up on key words and filling in the spaces based on the context of the conversation. This is similar to what I do when reading and is probably the way I deal with language in general. Sometimes this works fine, but sometimes I completely miss the point the speaker is trying to make.

One of the strategies I have developed to help keep me in conversations is to predict what the speaker will say. Since I am never exactly sure I will get the meaning right after I hear it, it makes more sense for me to try to think ahead of the speaker and figure out where he or she might be going with the conversation. This works well to a point, but sometimes I find myself jumping ahead to the wrong conclusion and having to back up and figure out where I got lost. Sometimes I do not know that I am on the wrong track until I get a strange reaction from the other person. Unlike many people with language problems, I am a talker, and it is rare that I do not participate fully in a conversation. I also like to draw analogies when listening because visualizing a concept helps me understand it better. I will sometimes make a comment or draw an analogy that immediately lets the listener know that I have misinterpreted what he or she has been trying to tell me. The speaker usually then explains once more, rewording the explanation in the process, allowing me a second chance to make the interpretation. People who know me usually give me analogies or examples of what they mean throughout their conversations.

Strangely enough, my problem does not show up as being severe on language tests in which I am asked to repeat a sentence word for word. I can complete a task such as this because I do not have to concentrate on the meaning of a sentence. I can repeat a sentence word for word if I am allowed to concentrate only on the word order. However, if I were asked to understand the meaning of that sentence, I most likely would be lost. An example of this would be if I were asked to repeat *and* comprehend the meaning of the sentence: *The boy who ate the ice cream got sick yesterday*; most likely I would repeat this sentence as *The boy got sick after eating ice cream*. In restructuring the sentence, I can perceive the idea and retain the meaning, but I lose some of the important facts. My language system overlooks the word *yesterday* as if it were not there. It is an important word that might be significant to the meaning of the sentence. Missing key words such as this has caused me problems both in and out of school. I have missed important information about homework assignments such as when they are due or how many pages a paper should be. I have also missed important information outside the school setting. Coaches are always throwing out information to swimmers which we have to keep track of in order to do a set of exercises. One problem I had when I was on the swim team was getting all the instructions my coaches would assign for practice. I would find myself picking up on the strokes that were involved and the order of the set, such as the length and distance, but I would miss the time intervals. I always had to get this information from my fellow pool junkies.

The most frustrating times for me are those when I am having trouble recalling words at the same time I am trying to figure out the order the words should go in a sentence. When this happens, I find myself getting really edgy. All the words and thoughts start spinning together in my brain and I feel like a hamster running on a wheel inside its cage. I am going nowhere but in circles. By the time I find the word I was searching for to begin with, I usually cannot find a place to insert it into my sentence. I usually start to mumble, and when I get puzzled looks from my listener, I know I am being unclear. Getting frustrated, I try to repeat the sentence, but I usually lose the word and the structure again and find myself in the same spinning circle. My only choice is to step off the spinning wheel completely and find a new way of expressing my thought. I usually find a simpler way to say what I mean, but I hate settling for less than the perfect way of expressing myself. Maybe it is because I have difficulty with language that I am so in tune with each and every word. I am aware that there are certain words that express exactly what I want to say, and those are the words I want to use. I have learned to slow my speech, allowing me time to search for my words and maintain the proper structure of the sentence, but sometimes I just have to stop, take a deep breath, and start over. There is no such thing as a casual conversation for me because I have to listen intently in order to comprehend the meaning of what the other person is saying to me, and I have to focus on finding every word I say in return and placing it in the sentence in the correct order. "Casual" conversations can make me tired and anxious, and if I allow the frustration to get to me, my self-concept suffers. However, I apparently fake these conversations pretty well, because few people recognize the fact that they are talking to someone with creative language abilities. They might think they are talking to someone from Boston . . . but that is another story.

Nonverbal communication

In my speech communication classes I learned that nonverbal communication plays a central part in human social behavior. Nonverbal social signals include gestures, body movements, posture, facial expression, gaze, proximity and spatial position, bodily contact, orientation, tones of voice, and other nonverbal aspects of speech, such as clothes and bodily adornment. Different messages are conveyed by different bodily signals: emotional states, attitudes to other people, information about the self. It supports speech by providing illustrations, feedback, and synchronizing signals. It is used as well in ritual and ceremony, art and music, propaganda and politics. An ability to properly interpret and convey nonverbal signals is essential for an individual to be accepted into society.

If verbal communication is my dragon, nonverbal communication is my sword. I understand its importance, and I know how to use it. Basically, I am good at reading people. I would consider nonverbal communication to be 80 percent of the way that I communicate. Most communication theorists estimate that nonverbal communication is between 60 percent and 65 percent for the average person.

I have developed the ability to understand the world around me from reading nonverbal signals and cues out of a sense of survival. In my world, spoken and written words held only distorted meanings. There was a point when I was younger that I gave up on words completely. By this I mean that I simply abandoned language and decided I did not need words. I treated the spoken word as having no value. If words had no value, it did not matter that I didn't understand them. By having no value, words could not defeat me. I did not like words and I refused to learn to deal with them. Instead, I began to match words to the way they were said. I learned to watch the faces of people who were speaking to me and of those who were listening with me. I could often fake understanding simply by copying the body language and facial expressions of the people around me. I learned to associate words with certain tones. For instance, I did not know the meaning of the words "drastically" or "rebel," but when they were spoken, I picked up a negative tone. I would cue into the intonation and not go any further. I hated school so much at this time anyway that I had gotten into the habit of purposely tuning the teacher out. It was not difficult to learn to look like I was listening while letting my mind run off into another world.

To this day I cue into intonation before I attend to the actual words being spoken. I have wondered if I would get more meaning from the sentences if I could ignore the tone of voice and concentraté only on the words. In experimenting with this idea, however, I find that I get lost in the words and have difficulty keeping my mind from drifting away from the person who is talking. I have decided that cuing in on the mood of the words helps me grab the key words better and consequently better understand the meaning of the sentence.

For example, if a teacher is giving out examples of test questions, the room is full of students furiously scribbling down the teacher's words. Because writing is so difficult for me, I would miss the major points if I were to follow the example of the other students. What I have learned to do is to write down occasional key words and phrases, but mostly concentrate on the teacher's voice tone, body gestures, and facial expressions. I've found that in doing this I am able to pick up and retain more information and more clues about what to study for the test.

When a teacher is lecturing, I try to concentrate on the mood, or tone, of the lecture to understand the meaning. In most cases I am successful, but sometimes I have misinterpreted the literal information given in the lecture because I have misinterpreted the mood. I have found myself on a completely different topic from the rest of the class in the middle of a class discussion. These are situations where understanding my creative learning abilities really pays off. My class notes are sketchy, but I know that because of my unique auditory abilities I cannot be sure that my understanding of the verbal message is clear to begin with. I compensate for my lack of notes by borrowing notes from a trusted friend. Notetakers are also provided by the university for students who have difficulties such as mine which interfere with their taking lecture notes.

Nonverbal communication also involves picking up information from pictures, so when teachers use visual aides in their lectures, I am much more likely to comprehend their words. I rely heavily on pictures, graphs, and maps to get meaning from both written and spoken language. I am very observant of diagrams and pictures and comprehend more from them than the words. I can distinguish shapes, colors, and textures of pictures much easier than I can recognize individual letters or words. On the first day of class, the teacher usually holds up the textbook and points out the name and author so we can buy the correct book. I would not remember the title of the book, but would recognize the book later because of a picture or other identifying visual information. I seem to block out the words and retain an image of the cover. I can seldom spell the title anyway, so when I go to buy the book, I search for it by the way it looks—the cover, the size, and the color.

When I have to rely solely on verbal information, I am at an uncomfortable disadvantage. I have a terrible time on the phone. I often find my attention drifting because I am usually so tuned in to watching and listening at the same time that I have difficulty concentrating when I only have words to listen to. Sometimes I find myself distracted by another person who walks by on my end of the line (especially if she's 5'5" and resembles Christie Brinkley) because I am pulled to "read" that person. Needless to say, messages can get confused if I am speaking to one person, but "reading" another. This results in a tendency to drift in and out of conversations, something which may appear to others to be a lack of attention to the conversation. This is not the case, however, because I have to focus attention more directly when I am on the phone to make up for the lack of visual cues. When I am on the phone, people often ask me if something is wrong, because my personality seems to be different. This happens partly because I rely on my own nonverbal ability to express myself. Instead of using words to let another person know I'm interested in what he or she is saying, I lift my eyebrows or nod my head. I cannot do this on the phone. On the phone, I am limited to verbal communication . . . words . . . language.

Nonverbal communication is an area that has been overlooked by parents and teachers and specialists. As I was growing up, much attention was paid to my verbal language problems; all of it was negative. If someone had only looked beyond the verbal deficits, they might have realized that I was learning to compensate by developing an ability to communicate nonverbally. It was not until college that I realized I was pretty good at figuring out people and what they were saying simply by watching them closely and tuning in to their moods. I feel that many individuals with language disabilities have a gift to look beyond the spoken word and advance to the empathic frontier. Do not underestimate their ability because of their written or oral language. Look closely and you may see an individual with an ability to read unwritten and unspoken language. This is a gift that needs to be encouraged. Just as a student who can write or speak well is encouraged to develop those skills, it is important that individuals with strong nonverbal skills be encouraged to develop and use those skills to overcome their language deficits. Their skill at nonverbal communication gives language-disabled individuals an edge that helps them stay afloat in a society where they lack equality in their own individual ways.

Making language work for me

Language has become important to me over the last few years. Only recently have I come to understand how my unique language abilities have interfered with my life, and through this understanding I have a new appreciation and love for language. This has happened in part because I have been blessed with a few teachers who have been able to reach within me and pull out their love of language through me. These teachers would read passages of literature aloud to the class. Then they would spend time dissecting and interpreting the meaning of the passages. They would make the words come alive in this one little passage until I not only learned to appreciate the literary meaning, I also gained a new understanding of the language itself.

This was the beginning. A new understanding of language was about to emerge. I began to learn how to interpret language for myself. I learned to form my own opinion of literature based on my past experiences. My English teachers had always discussed the deeper meanings of language, but the light alluded me, until one day, submerged in a sea of one-dimensional words, I listened as a teacher read a passage to me from a children's book. She was babbling on about two stuffed animals talking about what it would be like to be real rather than stuffed. I yawned and rolled my eyes back, but, being in the front row, I decided it was best to politely stay tuned in:

"What is REAL?" asked the Rabbit one day. . . . "Does it mean having things that buzz inside you and a stick-out handle?"

"Real isn't how you are made," said the Skin Horse. "It's a thing that happens to you. When a child loves you for a long, long time, not just to play with, but REALLY loves you, then you become Real."

"Does it hurt?" asked the Rabbit.

"Sometimes," said the Skin Horse, for he was always truthful. "When you are Real you don't mind being hurt."

"Does it happen all at once, like being wound up," he asked, "or bit by bit?"

"It doesn't happen all at once," said the Skin Horse. "You become. It takes a long time. That's why it doesn't often happen to people who break easily, or have sharp edges, or who have to be carefully kept. Generally, by the time you are Real, most of your hair has been loved off, and your eyes drop out and you get loose in the joints and very shabby. But these things don't matter at all, because once you are Real you can't be ugly, except to people who don't understand."

"I suppose you are Real?" said the Rabbit. And then he wished he had not said it, for he thought the Skin Horse might be sensitive. But the Skin Horse only smiled.

"The Boy's Uncle made me Real," he said. "That was a great many years ago; but once you are Real you can't become unreal again. It lasts for always." (*The Velveteen Rabbit*)

Taking in a deep breath I slowly began to realize there was a deeper meaning to what the teacher was saying. This passage was about more than stuffed animals discussing life in a toybox. The passage took on life without the teacher's dissection. As I evolved, my gills began to disappear. Slowly I realized I could hear the teacher better. Suddenly, I broke through the surface into a bright shining sun and inhaled a fresh sense of language. The one-dimensional passage that had been anchored to the bottom of the sea now belonged to me. Just as the Velveteen Rabbit eventually became real through the love of a boy, language became real for me through the love of a teacher. Until I heard this passage, I did not understand the beauty that words give to us.

Once I realized that language was multidimensional, I began to have fun with it. What had once been my enemy became my companion. I no longer hated language; however, I still was afraid of it. Since I no longer had gills, I could not allow myself to turn back. I had to keep swimming forward to the shore, picking up new words and meanings along the way. In order to realistically make it to the shore (graduate from college) I had to examine my language and come to terms with it. I felt like the favorite superhero of my youth, Aquaman. You see, Aquaman had to learn to communicate within the ocean environment in order to survive. He did this by learning the language of the sea. He used his aquapowers to communicate with the fish, but to be effective, he had to learn their language. Since I was now above water, I had to embark on the mission of learning my own language.

It is estimated that seventy-five percent of the students who have unique learning abilities have language problems. Many people might listen to me now and say I have no language problem because I have learned to handle it well. They would have to talk to me and ask me what is going on to really discover how hard I work to speak and to comprehend what is being said to me. I have come a long way in the last four years. I do much less groping for words now, and my vocabulary has multiplied more than I can say. I have also come to recognize my nonverbal communication ability for the strength that it is, and it has become a legitimate compensation strategy.

I listen to everything in pictures, meaning that I take

in sounds and put them into pictures. Some sounds appear to me in cursive, while others appear in print. Cursive is not as clear as print, so it is more difficult for me to understand. The cursive sounds are not necessarily less desirable, however. I have come to think of language as being like a business letter compared to a manuscript printed in Old English. The tone of a business letter is clearer and more direct. The letters are easier to see; however, the words used in a business letter are more boring and do not necessarily lend themselves to the formation of visual images. The language of the business letter is less frightening, but hardly exciting, and not necessarily easy to remember. The language that is written in Old English scares me. The words are very difficult to see (hear). However, if I take the time or get someone to help me to decipher the words, I find these passages much more exciting and richer in quality than the less frightening business letters. The words spoken in intonations difficult for me to distinguish are more exciting in the long run because once they become clear, they usually kick my brain into seeing pictures. Because the pictures are much more vivid, the points being made are easier to retain and comprehend. I believe this is why I always enjoyed classes such as literature, botany, and history more than my speech communication classes. In the speech communication classes, the lectures came through clearer because the words were in print and easier for me to hear, but they dealt with a lot of theories that were very difficult for me to retain. As in a business letter, there were few words given in the lectures that my brain could grab and make into a picture. Words that I cannot visualize have little meaning to me and lay no foundation on which to build. In my literature classes, on the other hand, the passages read to us by the teachers would come to me written in Old English. They were full of vocabulary words I did not understand and read by the teacher in dramatic intonations. Even though I had to struggle to understand what was being said, once I understood the words, I understood the meaning. This fact alone made it worth the struggle to understand.

Language that comes to me written in Old English seems to have more quality because there are more words that I can visualize. Even though the singsong voice or the dramatic voice intonations are harder for me to understand, they are more exciting. With the printed voice, you get what you see, but with the Old English voice, there is an invitation to explore further. Old English is like a jungle. The thought of entering is scary, but once I take the first step, I enter a world that vibrates with a life of its own. The colors are brighter and the potential for excitement is greater. It is scary, but I love it because it gives me more pictures. I have decided that trying to comprehend difficult language is worth taking that risk rather than trying to fake my way through.

People who know I have a language disability find it odd that I chose to major in speech communication. I'm not sure I was conscious of it at the time, but now I know that I did this in order to confront my flaw. In order to communicate the pictures within my brain, I had to learn how to use the spoken word. What I would like teachers, parents, and students to learn from my experiences is that people should not have to wait until they are almost adults to begin to understand their language systems. For years I received attention from specialists only because I had an articulation problem. I wish someone had realized and helped me understand that the basis of my learning difficulties lay in the fact that I use a different language system than most people. *I wish someone had taken the time to help me understand my system* and how it differed from the one most people use. *I wish someone would have worked with me to find my language strengths rather than trying to change my system to theirs.*

Teachers and parents should be on the look-out for red flags that could signal a language problem, and students with unique language abilities should work to understand their own language systems. Parts of their unique system may be good and used to their advantage, but many times the best communication choice will be to adapt to the system most people use. Children who have any type of articulation problems should be referred to language specialists to make sure basic language skills are not also impaired. Children who often stop and start over when trying to tell stories or pause for long periods between sentences may be having some problems with using words and sentences to express their thoughts. These are not symptoms that can be ignored. Children who do not follow instructions well may appear to have attention problems; however, they may be having difficulty with the language or they may be tuning out because they are giving up on understanding the words. Symptoms such as these may not be based in language, but the child needs to be assessed by a specialist to find out. Finally, any child who is having trouble learning to read or write should be evaluated to make sure that the difficulty does not lie with language. Language is the basis of academics. Children who cannot comprehend the spoken word cannot be expected to gain meaning from the written word. When a child is having learning difficulties, the first step is to accurately identify the problem. Only then can the correct solution be devised.

SIX

Math: A Different Language System

Math is a subject unlike reading, English, science, or social studies because it uses a different symbol system. While I have difficulty dealing with the alphabetical symbol system, the numerical system comes easier to me. I have little difficulty with the calculations involved in math, but the theories and concepts behind the calculations puzzle me. I understand individual pieces of this puzzle, but have difficulty fitting them into the whole concept of math and the part that numbers play in my life. I think part of my problem with learning math is that it has always been explained to me in words. Like everything else, math has its own vocabulary. Language is attached to the symbols that would be so easy to understand otherwise. Understandably, word problems have always been the most difficult for me. When I am listening to or reading a word problem, I sometimes leave out or reverse important information. While struggling through the words, I lose the meaning of the problem. I would like to go back and tell my teachers that I would have been able to do those math problems if they had helped me find a way to get through the language. I am not sure how this could have been done, however. I remember teachers drilling on certain language concepts—greater than and less than, for instance. They provided me with symbols (< and >) and a device to use in order to remember which way the symbol was to be turned (*"Think of it as an alligator mouth, Christopher. The alligator wants to eat* *the greatest amount of fish, so it will open its mouth wide."*) I didn't understand the analogy that teachers were trying to give me until I was several years into high school. Although I somewhat understood that the open alligator's mouth stood for the greatest amount, I did not connect that the less-than sign was the other end of the alligator's mouth. This should have been an easy concept for me because it was a picture, but when they started sticking more than one alligator mouth into a problem— 6 > 2 < 8, it really blew my mind. I could not figure out which number went with which mouth. I don't really know how I came to understand it. I just finally saw the light. Mathematical terms such as "greater than" and "less than" have always confused me even though I could easily tell you if a quantity of bananas was larger than another. I have learned that if I ignore oral or written explanations and simply concentrate on numerical examples, I can figure out and understand what is going on much quicker. This is because the other symbol system, language, is not getting in my way.

It is interesting that while I feel I am strong in math I do not enjoy it nearly as much as I do literature. This seems odd when you consider the fact that I have so much difficulty reading and writing. I like to think of math as a strength; it seems easier to conquer, so I make myself believe that. It seems to be something I can understand better than written language. It really bothers me to consider the fact that I am really not that great at math either. Throughout this book I have written about how difficult language is for me, both written and spoken. The fact is that all of the other subjects were such nightmares that they caused my momentum and excitement about learning to diminish every time I walked through the classroom door. Math, my "strong" subject, should have made me feel more at ease, but it is tied into the schoolroom setting and is an academic subject, and all academics are difficult. I probably have never given math a fair chance simply because it has always been associated with school.

Most of my problems with math have leaked out of the classroom into the real world, a fact I do not like. Math in the classroom is structured and applied to theoretical situations which I am supposed to take outside and use in a practical way. This has always confused me. Until recently I never realized that what the education system was trying to do was to enable me to take the concepts I learned in math *through language* and apply them to everyday situations. This is what math is all about, but I never made that connection. For instance, when measurements were discussed in class, my goal was simply to get through the measurement section in the book with a solid grade. I never comprehended that I would need this information outside the classroom. The examples being used by the teachers were practical examples, but I never seemed to realize that I would one day need to know this stuff to cook, or to build things, or to understand times and distances in track races. To me, math was just another school subject that was a little less demanding.

In second through fourth grade (which was four years because I repeated second grade) math was taught to me in the cubicle buildings in the back of the school away from the rest of the children. I don't remember receiving as much help in the special class with math, but it was included in the routine. My clearest memories are of using notecards to learn the times tables and concentrating on word problems. What bothers me is that I now know it was language that was crippling my understanding of math. I feel that if math had been presented to me more through pictures and diagrams, I would have had a much easier time understanding and holding on to the concepts. Instead of talking about measurements and giving them titles such as meter and inch, or quarts and gallons,

I think I would have been better off if my teachers had presented me with the basic problem of measurement—that there needs to be some standardized form of recognizing lengths and widths of objects or volumes of measure—and allowed me to come up with my own measurement system. The teacher could have filled a quart jar of water and a gallon jar of water and allowed me to see the difference in volumes. In doing this the teachers would have been assured that I understood the basic foundations of measurement and how measurement concepts fit into my everyday life. Once I had the basic concepts, then they could assign words to *my* concepts. Math is the one subject that does not rely solely on language, and teachers should take advantage of this with students like me who understand pictures and other nonverbal language better than the spoken or written word.

My problems with math were not as socially traumatizing as my problems with language because math was as difficult for others as it was for me. Math, unlike English, was not used everyday (at least not at that time in my life). You can get through a day without having to show that you know math, so I really did not feel like I was stupid in math. For this reason math was one subject I always put on a pedestal. When people asked me what my best subject was, I always said math. I knew that others around me were also struggling to learn math concepts, so it made it easier for me to accept the fact that I was not the only one struggling. My pedestal began to topple near the end of the fourth grade. This is when I went to battle with Mr. Multiplication. He was definitely a hard character to get to know. Although his concepts were easily understood, his troops were too numerous to deal with.

Even at this early age I knew I was dealing with a different type of problem. Writing and reading were my major problems and had been the primary cause of my faking throughout school. This was the first time I realized that my *memory* was also a problem. Of course at the time I could not put a label on it; as usual I simply assumed that my stupidity had leaked into my math class. As much as I practiced my tables, I had trouble recalling them on demand. All of Mr. Multiplication's troops seemed to be well advised in the technique of camouflage. The closer I looked for them in my mind, the harder they were to find. It was almost as if I was telling myself I didn't want to face (learn) them.

At this time the only reason I went to school was because I was forced to go. I had no goals or ambitions. I had no interest in anything we did. All of my energy went into "faking it," covering up the fact that I was stupid. Mr. Multiplication confused me, and I didn't want anyone to know. I did not want to face the fact that math was giving me difficulty, so I learned enough to get by. I could memorize the tables long enough to pass a test, but they would not stick with me. I was subjected to embarrassment because I *thought* I was the only person in the entire class who didn't know Mr. Multiplication's troops. When I was called on in class, I always seemed to miss them. The other kids really did not seem to care, but *I did.* I could get the weapons out and use them, but I had no battle strategy, so I never won. I managed to stay in the war until the end of the fourth grade, but not without scars. Then I went into hand-to-hand combat with the Mr. Multiplication's troops.

In the classroom, toward the end of the fourth grade, we had battles against each other. We were divided into two teams, and one person from each team had to go to the board and work the same double-digit multiplication problem. Whoever finished first won a point for his or her team. I could not do the problems because I did not know my tables. I had been able to fake it up until this time, but for the first time, I felt that Mr. Multiplication might win the war.

During the math battles, it was evident that I was much slower than everyone else. I'm not sure if this was because I actually knew less than the person I was up against or because I felt inferior since I was competing in an academic subject, a symbol of failure. At the mention of math battles, my stomach began to churn, and my hands got sweaty. I could hardly keep a grip on my weapon.

The numbers and the problems I was given in these battles constantly changed. I didn't know what Mr. Multiplication would throw at me next, so there was no way to prepare. I now feel that if I had known what the problems were, I could have memorized the solutions, so I wouldn't have to do the calculations on the spot. (This was usually my way of faking things. Instead of learning information, I would memorize it for short periods of time.) I have always felt that people should prepare themselves before a battle rather than blindly march onto the battlefield at night. The multiplication battles were being fought at night, and were not situations I could control.

As an adult I can relate that time in my life to going through my first job interviews. In an interview, I never knew what the questions would be or what the interviewer would be like. The interviewer might try to put me on the spot or make it easy for me. Both situations deal with faking it. At the interview, the prospective employee must appear to be confident and in control. If this is not achieved, there is a good chance that the job will be denied.

I did not truly confront my enemy using all of my battle strategies and weapons until I was almost through with the fifth grade. I was determined not to let Mr. Multiplication scar me any further. I was also about to enter a new school and thought this would be an opportunity to get a fresh start. Somehow I knew I could win this war, even though my war with words had been lost long before. I spent the summer before fifth grade concentrating on learning my multiplication tables. Since they were numbers, I found that I could see them clearly in my mind. Once I determined that I was going to *learn* them for life rather than *memorize* them for a test, I seemed to be able to place them into a deeper, more secure part of my brain where they could not escape so easily. I did this by picturing them rather than relying on the rhymes we had practiced so much in school. Now I understand that the multiplication records and the classroom drills that we repeated over and over in a singsong voice (one-times-one-is-one; one-times-two-is-two, etc.) did not fit my unique learning abilities. These drills were presented in a format that was totally auditory—words that were even more distorted by a singsong presentation. When I stopped trying to memorize the tables by saying them over and over in my mind as I had been taught to do, I began to make sense of them and therefore, to learn them. I used cards with the equations printed on one side and the answers on the other. I could learn them in privacy without worrying about the words that went with the numbers.

Today I still have trouble with my multiplication tables if only words are used. Just recently one of my teachers was trying to make a point about things that come automatically to us. "For example," he said, "if I asked 'What is three times four?' everybody would be able to answer automatically without thinking . . ." Well, I was not able to answer automatically, and I was suddenly seized with the fear that he would call on me to give this "automatic" answer. When I wrote the problem on my paper ($3 \times 4 =$), I knew the answer immediately; I just had to visualize it first. This is why I am no longer bothered by Mr. Multiplication in my math classes. There are no more competitions or auditory drills. I simply have to perform the operation in front of me without giving an explanation. Of course *now* we have calculators. . . .

Other than memorizing the multiplication facts, I feel that most of my math problems really come from my difficulty with language and being unable to tie the calculations I was learning to the concepts behind them. I realize now that just as the word "math" is broken down into letters—M-A-T-H—the system of math is taught in different segments. However, these segments seemed to be completely individualized and unconnected to me as a child. Every year the class would go through a math book in a certain sequence, usually learning addition first, then subtraction, multiplication, and division, in that order. Sometimes we progressed into the latter chapters that dealt with measurement, time, fractions, and geometry, but by this time we were nearing the end of the year and summer was on the minds of both students and teachers. We crammed the entire last few chapters of the book into the last few weeks of school. The next year we would start over with the same routine—the same movie with different actors. What I found curious about this is that the script never changed, and the acts in the play were never connected. There was never a conclusion or a final scene, except for a grade, if that can be considered a conclusion. We all know that a grade is not a true reflection of what was learned in class. We, the actors, were really good at the first two acts (addition and subtraction) and not too bad at acts three and four (multiplication and division), but we hardly knew our lines for the last few acts (time and measurement, fractions, geometry), and never saw the reason for making the movie in the first place.

I can look back and say that it would have been very helpful if my teachers had tied each chapter to the ones we had learned before so that I could better understand the connections. Math, as a subject, never seemed to be connected to anything else. It was not tied to anything I did outside of school, and it seemed to be not even connected to itself. I understand now that there are all kinds of connections in math and that each step builds on the one before it; however, as a child these connections were never made clear to me. Teachers need to remember that students may not see the logic of math. They may not comprehend the whole picture or tie the concepts together. They also will not ask questions. I know there were many times in school that I had questions but did not feel comfortable asking them. Whether they intend it or not, teachers can be intimidating. They do not seem to realize how hard it is for students to show that they do not understand something that everyone around them seems to know. (Even when teachers say, "Don't be afraid to ask questions." or "How can you learn, if you don't ask questions?") Many times I would not allow myself to wonder about the new things I was learning in school because I was afraid. If I allowed myself to consider how much there was to learn, I would realize the effort I would have to make. I imagine many children find it overwhelming to realize how much they really do not know, so they are not going to risk that feeling by asking questions. Having questions answered usually leads to more questions! Somehow teachers need to provide a doorway for students to get out of their comfort zones. I know now that it is fun to wonder about things and that dreams and goals come from leaving the comfort zone and allowing your mind to be free. In elementary school math classes, however, it was much more comfortable to simply sit and do my calculation problems and not wonder about how they related to my *real* life—the enjoyable part of life—outside of school.

It would have been so easy for me to relate math to my real life because athletics is full of mathematical concepts. In all of my dealings with time and measurement in swimming and track I never made the connection that *this* was math. Being involved in athletics for most of my life, I was constantly surrounded by time and measurement. Not only did I have to be at practice at certain times each day, my performance was measured strictly by distance and time. The first formula that ever made sense to me was Time + Distance = Performance. It is very important for an athlete to understand the concepts of time. While many of my teammates in swimming were fighting to lower their times, I found myself not so concerned with time as with competition. As with so many other things, I think I comprehended time differently from those around me. Most of my fellow athletes were able to spit out different times with ease; whether discussing great workout times or meet times, they were able to retain and comprehend the time concepts a lot better than I was. I think I actually had an inner sense of time, but I could not retain the meaning of time as it was explained through language. For instance, I had trouble keeping world record swim times straight in my head, whereas most of my teammates not only knew all the record times but also who the record holders were. These were important topics of conversation around the pool, an important part of my social life at the time. It was easier to compete physically with my friends than to maintain a social conversation.

I always felt like I was stupid because I could not retain or fully comprehend the time concepts. I remember looking at time cards and being very confused about the way seconds were recorded. Understanding time is very important in swimming because cut-off times come down to tenths and hundredths of seconds. I still do not understand why a tenth is larger than a hundredth. This concept puzzles me and it still takes me a second to put the pieces together. I always knew the cut-off times I had to make to be good, but I really did not *comprehend* their meaning. When I got together with other swimmers and everybody was talking about the different times they swam, I had trouble staying in the conversations because I had difficulty relating my times to theirs.

I also had trouble with time outside of athletics. To this day I force myself to wear a watch with hands because using a digital watch is too easy. Understand that I am not into making things harder for myself. I wear a watch with hands because if I did not, I would soon forget how to tell time on these types of clocks. The world has not yet gone entirely digital, and being able to read a clock with hands is necessary in everyday life. I was in high school before I actually accomplished this feat, and I am not about to lose it. I think a clock with hands actually makes it easier to understand the concept of time better than a digital watch. People with unique learning abilities who wear digital watches might save face on occasion because they can immediately report the time when asked by a friend and be sure that the words they speak accurately reflect the numbers on their watches. However, I know many people who do not understand what those words actually mean in relation to time. The vocabulary words used to tell time—second, minute, hour, day, week, year, century, before, after—were difficult for me to learn, but the concepts behind them are even more difficult and must be practiced. I am not saying that digital clocks are bad. They are great tools. They light up and are clear. But they were becoming my crutch, so I made myself get to know "the little hand and the big hand" once again.

Measurement in time was not the only math skill related to athletic competition; we also had to understand measurement in distance. When I was very young, before I started swimming, I ran and jumped on different school track teams. I was considered to be pretty good compared to my peers. In fact my times were ranked with the best in my age group. A problem I had in dealing with track, however, was comprehending the different races I had to run. Distance on the track was very difficult for me to perceive. I always had trouble matching up the given yards with the distance to be run. For instance, I never made the connection that the 220 race was half the distance of the 440. This should have been easy for me to understand because running the 440 meant running all the way around the track, while running the 220 meant running only halfway around. But the starting points were at different places on the track, and no one ever helped me make the connection as to how these two races were related. I guess teachers and coaches assume that something so obvious to them must also be obvious to their students or that making such a connection one time is enough. Learning for a child comes in pieces. I learned about fractions in math class, and I learned how to run two different kinds of races from my track coach. What I did not have as a child was the ability to see the relationship between these two pieces of information. Understanding their relationship would have helped me in track as well as in school. I might even have gained a better appreciation for how the things I was doing in school could help me outside of school. But no one drew those connections for me or taught me to draw them for myself for many years. To this day I don't worry about how many yards or meters a swimming race is because I think of the races in terms of laps.

I love sports, and it bothers me that my difficulty attaching language to numerical information sometimes interferes with my understanding of the games and the players, and sometimes my social interaction with others. In college I always had trouble matching the football players with their numbers. When I would look down on the field, my friends would be talking about a player by his number, and I would be lost. I knew him by his name, but couldn't identify him by his number. It did not matter that only two-digit numbers were involved; the players might as well have had their social security numbers on their backs. I believe the problem here was similar to my battles with Mr. Multiplication and my inability to attach sounds to letters. In my language system there seems to be no logical reason to give names to letters and numbers. With numbers I am able to keep up for a time, but after a point there seems to be too many words to keep up with. When I am trying to simply remember the name that goes with a number, it is almost impossible to make the third step and remember a number that goes with each player. Although being unable to remember football players' numbers is not a life-threatening situation, it helps me to understand why I have difficulty. Not only do I feel less stupid (the fact that my friends do not have the same creative learning abilities as I do is *their* loss), but it also helps me think ahead to similar situations so that I can be ready with compensation strategies.

I was able to conquer upper level math courses, such as algebra, statistics, calculus, and trigonometry because I had help in understanding how my unique learning abilities affect my ability to learn math, allowing me to develop the strategies that got me through the classes. Language was a tremendous problem for me in these upper level courses. When introducing new concepts, my college math teachers would usually "walk through" a sample problem. These examples are designed to provide a foundation for understanding an abstract mathematical concept. New language concepts are also introduced as the problems are explained. Rather than "walking through" examples, my teachers would run. They would introduce a new mathematical concept by quickly going over one example, using mathematical terminology I had never heard before. Not only did I have to struggle to comprehend the new concept, but also the new words. As the teachers turned their backs to the class and wrote a string of numbers and symbols on the blackboard, speaking in a language none of us understood, I sometimes took pleasure in knowing that I was not the only person in the class who was lost. Math teachers do not seem to realize that it is important for students to have the basic math concepts *before* new terminology is introduced. Statistics is a terrific example. The teachers would introduce statistical concepts right from the beginning by using the new language. It is like trying to learn math in a foreign language. If students have never been exposed to statistical vocabulary before entering the classroom, there is a good chance they will become lost on the first day. I successfully completed these higher level courses only because my LD specialist understood that I was missing the basic concepts. A person builds on what is already known by using language skills, but it is essential to have a strong base of math concepts before new language is introduced. When teachers use a new language to introduce new concepts, the foundation is weak and the building crumbles.

The real math foundation should be built long before a student reaches college or even high school, and I do not think this can be done by staying in the classroom and performing the same play year after year. I think students need more opportunities to see math in action. For instance, by taking a trip to the bank to understand the concept of interest; inviting a construction worker into class to show how math is used on the job; having a market day where students have to cook or make things and sell them to other students; holding an auction and letting the students figure the value of each object; building the props for a play. There are so many things that can be done to put math into action that it doesn't make sense to make actors face the same script year after year, only to read it, but never to act it out. Students need to be allowed to experience learning. The "standard method" for teaching, say, math will not be successful with all students. Even "normal" students are not all "standard." And those of us with unique learning abilities, while not "normal" or "standard," are fully capable of learning when the subject is presented on our level.

SEVEN

Private Pain

Private Pain

As I sit here, a rush of pain comes over me.
Then the sadness and depression set in.
You do not understand why I am sad.

I cry today for all the things I should have done.
I cry for all those things I must still do.
These things may seem simple or even trivial to the
    average person.
To me they are life and death.
I am possessed with drive to succeed when I could
    say, "I cannot"
I *must* strive to overcome this thing.

You may never know why I weep, or even that I do.
Please, just be there for me when I feel I must do
    more than cry.

Elizabeth Baily
a creative learner

When I first began to face my academic difficulties and accepted the fact that college would be a struggle for me, I focused only on the academic aspects of my problems— the "learning" part of "learning disabilities." I was not prepared for the emotional drain on my energy that came from dealing with the day-to-day academic stresses and from being in a social environment in which reading and writing were standard means of communication. My senior year was my fifth year in college. I had mastered the study skills and compensation strategies that helped me get through my classes, but I was burned out to the point that I seriously considered dropping out. I did not think I could explain to one more teacher why I would need to take my tests on a computer, or figure out one more scheme to hide from my classmates the fact that I received special modifications. Facing another year of hours on end of studying with little time for play was almost more than I could imagine. All I wanted to do was get away from everything. Taking a bicycle tour of Europe was a fantasy that kept playing in my mind. It was not the academic challenges that almost kept me from getting my degree, but rather the social and emotional stress of living with a learning disability. Too often, emphasis is placed on the academic side of learning disabilities, and the rest of the human being is forgotten. Professionals and parents concentrate all of their energies on helping us get through school, sometimes forgetting that the academic difficulties may be the least of our problems and that our unique way of seeing and hearing will not end with a high school or college diploma.

The poem at the beginning of this chapter was written by a friend of mine. Elizabeth writes about what many students with learning disabilities feel as they go through school. Through my experiences in meeting and talking with other students like me, I have developed my own theory which I have named my ABC Social Seesaw Theory. It considers the social and emotional ups and downs of living with unique learning abilities. *A* is for Achieving, *B* is for Balancing, and *C* is for Cwitting (the way quitting *should* be spelled!). Elizabeth's poem represents the *A* (achieving) LD personality. These students are usually the ones who will strive to be the very best they can be. They will set goals and replace them with higher goals before the first goals are achieved. They will never be satisfied with second best. They usually spend much time organizing, making plans, and setting goals, even though this is not always evident to others. They are self-motivated and driven to the point that they cannot relax. They are never satisfied with what they are and never accept their handicap. They also bite their fingernails a lot.

The B student is a balanced individual. These students appear to be more laid back. Their anxiety and drive is not particularly detectable in their personalities. They have a sense of achievement, but it is not all consuming. They are reasonably satisfied with most passing grades. It does not seem to bother them as much as the A's that their grades do not reflect the amount of effort they put in. They are satisfied with the tools they are given in life and seem to accept themselves as they are.

The C students "cwit" before giving themselves a chance. For whatever reason, they give up. They sometimes find outlets outside of school. For instance, they might direct their energies toward a girlfriend or boyfriend, or they might be the class clown or the school behavioral problem. They feel inferior in the classroom, so entertain themselves with other diversions rather than using their energy for education. Some have given up completely and label themselves complete failures. Their attitude is not due only to their own personalities. It is a two-sided issue. Part of their failure comes from the lack of motivation and encouragement given in the educational process. Unlike the A's and B's, the C's choose to let the negative reinforcement of academic experience rule their lives. They will not allow themselves to take control because of their *fear of failure*. Students who spend their lives receiving only negative reinforcement become people in the working world who have no sense of self-empowerment. They go through their lives talking about what they could have done and been. Somewhere along the line people choose to either face their weaknesses and meet the challenge or they choose to deny these weaknesses by convincing themselves that schoolwork is not for them.

Academic education is a process of learning and expanding one's self. The C's believe they are no good in school. They *know* they are stupid. There is no faking it. They do not see that it is worth their efforts to try to be something they believe they cannot be.

I know about *A* people because I am one. I can relate to Elizabeth's poem because I have felt the same feelings. The line that I relate to most is: "I am possessed with drive to succeed when I could say 'I cannot.' " The energy that comes from within myself has helped me through college and four years of swimming. Even though this drive to succeed has been good for me, it has also had its downfalls. I often have trouble sleeping simply because I cannot relax. My mind is always working, and I constantly push to stay on top of things in order to feel confident. Elizabeth writes that some of the things that are important to her may seem trivial to the average person. Setting a goal of *C* in a class, for instance, may seem to show a lack of motivation to the student who would have to put out little effort to obtain that score. To people who have been told all their lives that they should never even attempt college, a *C* is as good as a gold medal.

I have named my theory the *ABC Social Seesaw* because life is a particularly delicate balancing act at best, and for individuals who are somewhat different from society's "norm," things can be even more precarious. I see the *B*'s as being the most content and stable of all of us. The *B*'s are the fulcrum in the seesaw. They are able to balance the ups and downs of their lives. The *C*'s and *A*'s, being on extreme ends of the seesaw, have more tendencies to fall off. Elizabeth acknowledges this in the last line of her poem: "Please, just be there for me when I feel I must do more than cry." Elizabeth explained to me that she is talking about suicide in this line and that it is more of a reality for her than most people think. People see her as a fighter, and would never believe she has entertained thoughts of suicide. She is asking for two things in the last line of the poem: one, to catch her before she falls off the seesaw, and the other, to understand that falling is a possibility she might choose.

Suicide is not something people easily talk about, and sometimes we may find ourselves avoiding the topic. It is something, however, that must be acknowledged and faced. A friend of mine once said that people with learning disabilities cannot help but have some kind of emotional problems. Having the intelligence to understand exactly how different you are from others makes life very difficult at times. Dealing with having a learning disability may not be overwhelming in itself, but added to the average social pressures and problems we all face daily, it could be enough of a factor to make a person choose to fall off the Seesaw. My friend who made this statement fell off. His learning disabilities were not the major cause of his frustration with life, but they played a part. His falling was a tremendous shock to Elizabeth and me because we had looked up to him as someone who was really together and dealt well with his problems. He often joked around and made light of his creative spellings and being unable to find books in the library because he did not know the alphabet. None of us guessed how serious life really was for him. Sometimes "faking it" is not a healthy way to live.

Because of the emotional challenges, it is important for people with learning disabilities to learn and understand as much as possible about their unique abilities so they can deal with how their lives are affected. They must strive to head toward the fulcrum of the seesaw. They will probably never reach perfect balance, but they can find security, stability, and contentment. Everyone feels down from time to time when the Seesaw begins to tilt. This is when it is important to find someone to talk to that they trust will understand, who will take them by the hand and lead them back toward the fulcrum.

My emotional state affects my ability level. When an athlete performs, his or her state of mind is very important and often dictates the outcome of the competition. For instance, tennis players can spend hours playing one match. During this match the emotional states of the players fluctuate. The emotions can range from a very high state after a fantastic volley to a very low state after a bad call. State of mind can determine momentum for an entire game. Emotional state is proven to make a difference in athletic competition. What I would like to explore here is how students' emotional states can affect their performance in class. Every time students with unique learning abilities walk through a classroom door, they are already facing an emotional low point because of the overwhelming challenge of academics and the possibility that one of their peers will see through their mask and think that they are stupid. It sometimes takes every ounce of energy to perform simple classroom tasks, and if anything else is going on in that student's life, classroom performance can be affected. Teachers often complain that students with learning disabilities work very inconsistently. One day they can do everything requested of them while the next day they cannot spell or read the same material they did the day before. This can happen because there are times that the student simply does not have the energy or concentration required to function at one hundred percent. While other students can work consistently with eighty percent effort, the student with unique learning abilities needs to be functioning at full capacity. I wish teachers would realize the difference they can make in students' classroom performances simply by understanding this fact rather than reinforcing the problem by saying, "You knew how to do this yesterday!"

Teachers who take the time to ask might find out why
the student is distracted, and it is important to give the
student as much positive feedback as possible in order
to keep the student's emotional level high.

I find that one of the most emotional experiences for
me comes when I am taking tests. At these times I am
placed in a situation in which I have to show my weaknesses for a grade. For example, I recently took a classics
test that was more challenging than I had expected. I had
studied the material and knew I understood it. When the
test was put in front of me, however, I noticed that the
first ten questions were fill-in-the-blanks. I immediately
put up my guard. I got frustrated because I could not
remember what the answers looked like, even though I
knew what they were. I had practiced learning these
words the night before by writing them over and over. I
was trying to learn how to recognize them and differen-
tiate between the ones that started with the same letter.
(Classical literature seems to contain an unusual number
of words that look alike! In the story of *Aeneas*, for example, the hero's father is *Anchises*, his son is *Ascanius*,
and his armor bearer is *Achates*. Even people who can
distinguish individual letters must have trouble keeping
these names straight!) I did not expect to have to spell
these words because I thought the test was going to be
multiple choice. When I got the test and saw that it was
short answer, I became tense because I knew I would have
to find a way to hide the fact that I could not spell these
words. I had a prearranged agreement with the teacher
that she would not count off for spelling, so I wasn't worried about that. I was concerned, however, that I might
not get close enough to the correct spelling that she would
be able to recognize the word. As my anxiety increased,
my concentration clouded. All the words I had practiced
writing the night before began to jumble together in my
brain. All the *P* words began to look just like all the *C*

words. My eyes wandered to the rest of the test. By the time I got to number eleven, I was emotionally very tense. I was also very conscious of the people around me. I was not concerned that someone might look on my paper to cheat, but more that they would do this and discover that I was writing in some unknown language. By this time it looked like Japanese. My performance on the rest of the test did not demonstrate my knowledge of the material. The further I went, the fewer words I could distinguish (read) or spell. By the end of the test my correct answers were few and far between. For some people the agony would be over with the taking of the test. I knew, however, that I still had to face the grade—a grade that did not at all reflect my knowledge of the subject or the hours I had studied.

When taking tests, I have to deal first with the teacher and then with my classmates. As I was taking this test, I felt I was dealing personally with the teacher because I had to write so she could read my answers and because I knew she would see the results and think I had not studied at all. I liked this teacher and enjoyed the class and was disappointed in myself that the test would not reflect either my feelings or my knowledge. I felt as if I were letting the teacher down.

When the graded tests were handed back the next day, my second chore was dealing with the students around me. Not only was my grade lower, but most of the words on my test were spelled wrong. I was nervously trying to hide these two facts from my fellow students. I quickly discovered that the student beside me (who I had worried might try to cheat off my paper) had made a 98. He had obviously not lifted any answers from *my* paper because I made a 75 (a passing grade, but not the grade I could have earned). Leaning over to peer at my paper, my classmate said, "I missed number four. Do you know what the correct answer should be?" Fortunately, this was one I had answered correctly, so I turned to the front page to give him the answer. As soon as he asked me, I knew I was going to have trouble. My emotions flared not only because I was being called on to read the answer, but also because I was showing him all the red marks that decorated my mistakes. The tension came back, this time worse than it had been the day before. I was openly showing my disability to one of my peers. I fumbled through the pages, and it felt like my hands were shaking. I looked at the word in front of me: Cato. I panicked because I could not read it. My emotions would not allow me to read this word. At that moment the word could have been Cato or Cicero or Caesar, all the C words that I had practiced two days before. I quickly faked it, and blurted out "Caesar," knowing somehow that it was not right. The guy looked away. I took a deep breath and looked at the word again and read it right. I corrected my mistake and told him it was "Cato." What this incident demonstrates is that when faced with different emotional circumstances, just like hitting a bad serve in tennis, a person has to be able to take a deep breath and move on. Just as athletes have to show their opponents that one mistake is not going to defeat them, academically troubled students must understand what is happening and learn to deal with their emotions. Just as athletes put restraints on their emotions, students must learn that as difficult as some experiences are, they must be able to learn from them and move on.

It is also important to learn to deal with the emotional factors caused by learning disabilities outside of the classroom. Because the word "learning" is attached to the word "disabilities," many people associate the problem only with school. I have spoken to parents whose children are struggling in elementary school. Many times they do not want to accept the fact that their child's problems reach beyond the classroom. They don't want me to tell them

that some of my most difficult moments have occurred
during everyday events. In fact, it is often in such "normal" times as parties and celebrations that I am caught
off guard and hit with problems I had not anticipated. I
have learned to be better prepared for these occasions,
particularly after several things that have happened to me
since I have been at college.

No birthday has ever compared to the one I had during
my freshman year. The fact that it was my first year at a
major university and that I had just finished a great year
of swimming made this the best birthday ever—more exciting than any that had preceded it. Everybody seemed
to know it was my birthday. Everywhere I went I ran into
people who wished me a happy birthday. A group of
friends got together and decorated my room with pictures
of not-so-modest females. A friend took me out to lunch.
It was my perfect birthday—until I was asked to read my
birthday cards aloud in front of a room full of people. I
tried to get out of it by joking around, but when a person
is surrounded by a bunch of friends, the peers usually
have the advantage. They insisted, and I had to give in.
I started reading, stumbling through verses that were
supposed to rhyme and clichés that were supposed to
make me blush. Instead of enjoying the moment, I became
frustrated and my face grew warm. I tensed up, and my
mood switched from delight to apprehension. In looking
back, I feel that the situation probably was not as bad as
I felt it was at the time. I realize now that the cards were
not the barrier; it was my mind. Ingrained in me was the
fear of reading aloud, especially reading aloud on the spot.
The cards could have been as easy to read as "Jane ran
over the hill," but I still would have been tense, and my
face would still have gotten warm. Even though I have
trouble reading, it would not have been as bad as I made
it out to be if I had stopped and taken a deep breath

instead of trying to fake it and pretend that I could not read the cards because I was embarrassed.

Other social occasions that have given me unanticipated difficulty have been those surrounding the traditions that are so often present on college campuses, especially among athletes. Traditions are sometimes thought of as exciting and sometimes as boring. For me, traditions can be scary. I had to face one of those scary traditions each Christmas break during the four years I was on the Georgia swim team. The story goes something like this:

The end of fall quarter comes quickly. Students are usually seen rushing to their cars after final exams. However, in looking closely at the campus, one would see that there are a few students who remain. These are the athletes. They are not allowed to go home for more than a week and a half after everyone else has been thoroughly entrenched in the Christmas rush. For the swimmers, this time of year is looked forward to only when one has a broken arm. This is the hardest part of training for most college swimmers. Rather than remaining on campus, our team heads for Florida for a week of intensive training. By the end of the week, everybody is drained and unable to lift their arms. Their noses are red and running from the cold wind and water that they submerge their bodies in for seven hours each day. The end of the week signals the time for an age-old University of Georgia swimming tradition—Gag Awards Night.

Preparation for this night begins at the first of the week when every swimmer draws another swimmer's name (only male swimmers participate in this). The name of the game is to cut down, or "rag," another swimmer. This is done by picking a flaw, a weakness, or a touchy point, such as a girlfriend, and writing a clever, but mean poem about this item and giving it along with a gag gift to the person whose name was drawn. On the last night of the week each swimmer stands up and selects the gift that was chosen for him and reads the accompanying poem aloud. As one can quickly see, a tradition such as this which involves both reading and writing could have been the downfall of my social and emotional well-being. We were staying in a motel, so it was difficult for me to obtain a dictionary. I had to ask a friend, one of the female swimmers, for help. During my freshman year, I did not really think things through yet and thought the worst was over after I had written my poem. It did not occur to me until that night that I was going to have to read *my* poem aloud in front of all of my peers. This terrified me. What I did not realize at the time was that having to read aloud was not the worst thing that would happen to me that night. The person who had drawn my name did not know me very well, so decided to use the only thing he knew about me that he could pick on—the fact that I entered the university through the developmental studies program. So as I stood up in the traditional manner, perched upon a chair, I found myself facing the audience trying not to let them see my flaw—my poor reading— while I was reading a poem about the very flaw I was trying to hide. The poem was cleverly written to imply that I was a "dumb jock"—stupid. Without knowing me well at all, the swimmer had given a blow to my self-esteem that I will never forget. A physical blow to my abdomen would have been easier to take.

Because this was my freshman year, I was facing a new situation and feeling my way around. People had been forming their opinions about me throughout this first quarter, and the manner in which I handled this situation would further influence their opinions of me. Their opinions were very important to me, so I knew I had to get through this somehow. I did it by faking it. I read slowly and stopped frequently to laugh. I was laughing as I was reading it, which helped to cover up some of the stumbling over words. I was laughing because I knew I had to and not because of what the words said. In this instance, the words were harder to read because they were cutting rather than because they all looked alike. Getting through this incident helped me prepare for the three traditional Gag Award Nights to come.

Social situations like this cannot be avoided. People with and without unique learning abilities are going to have to face uncomfortable social situations in their lives. It may be giving a speech, making a class presentation, or participating in school traditions, but there will come a time when everyone will have to face his or her peers. Throughout this book I have talked about how faking it can affect one's self-concept in a negative way. The fact is that it is sometimes necessary to fake things. The trick is acknowledging when you're faking and when you're not. This is a fine line that must be recognized. There is no way around it. Peers can be cruel, but they must be dealt with. When faced with situations in which one has to show flaws to peers, whether it be reading, writing, or speaking, sometimes it is necessary to fake it. This is when the person with creative learning abilities can reach inside and use that creativity to bring out the actor that is used throughout life with parents and teachers.

Everybody plays different roles from time to time. When kids ask their fathers for money, they play different characters than when they ask their mothers. Whenever possible we must prepare for social situations and antic- ipate what might happen and how we will act. For ex- ample, we all know that in our lives we may be asked to read birthday cards in front of our friends. People with unique learning abilities should do their homework now, before it happens. This means imagining a situation, going over it internally, and deciding whether to be honest or if it is a situation that can be *legitimately faked*, per-

haps suggesting that it might be more effective for someone else to read the cards—the group extrovert or class
clown, for example. Or doing like I have done: laughing
as I stumble over the words, covering my mistakes. Being
creative and preparing now is the best way for creative
learners to confront these situations.

   Another thing we have to deal with is younger people
who have better academic skills than we do, who *appear*
to be brighter than we are. When a child can sound out
words better than I can, my self-image is attacked. For
instance, I have a cousin, Blake, who is eight years old,
an eight-year-old with the intellect of a twelve-year-old.
Given a word, he can usually not only sound it out and
pronounce it perfectly, but he also comprehends its meaning. He is an eight-year-old child who cannot only read
the word "ambiguous," but knows what it means. I discovered this when Blake came across this word when
reading a newspaper article to me. As he opened his
mouth, his lips moved in an awkward manner. I could
tell by looking into his eyes that his mind was working.
He attacked the word as if he were in the Daytona 500.
Driving a car named *Success*, his mind was on wheels as
he maneuvered his car in and out of the other race cars,
rubbing against each fender he passed. He was almost
there. With a final push on the accelerator, his mind broke
free, and the word "ambiguous" raced out of his mouth.

   A fire child, Blake leaves his brand on each track he
races. His future can only be seen from the winner's circle.
The only thing higher than his achievement will be the
trophy above his head. He is a winner. His future only
has to be driven to be successful. Sometimes I ask myself
where I was at this point in life. I was an eight-year-old
child who could barely read, who could not spell, and
would not have attempted to figure out the word "ambiguous." I was not driving the same car, *Success*. My car
was given the name *Questionable*. How did my teachers,

my parents, and my friends view my future? Did they see me in that same winner's circle or just hope that I could finish the race? Were they as optimistic about me as they are about Blake? I did not have the same tools that Blake has, so how could they expect the same results from me? But more importantly, how could I expect the same results Blake does of himself? What was my self-image at that time compared to Blake's? At eight years of age I seemed to be trapped. Academics were not on my side. My parents did what they could to make me understand that I was smart and that I could be a winner, but the feedback I was receiving from the race announcer was that I was in last place.

Sometimes I ask myself how I came from last place to being a recognized driver. I was lucky. I had a good pit crew. Someone to change my wheels when they were bare. Someone to tune up my engine when it was running rough. Most importantly, I had someone to pat me on the hood and talk to me and give me confidence. I was not a Blake when I was eight years old. I was a Christopher. With different tools, a different car, trying to win a different race. My destiny was not to be a lawyer or a doctor, but to be an educator of parents, and teachers, and students who were given the same tools I had when I was eight. So my instructions are to parents and teachers: Do not let these students quit the race no matter how slow their cars and no matter how many times they wreck their cars. And my advice to the student is: If your pit crew is not giving you the backup you need, educate them. Let them know your frustrations and work with them to form a plan that will get you into the winner's circle.

I cannot lie. It is frustrating to see other cars around me that appear to perform better. When someone ten years younger than I can easily read material with which I have to struggle, it makes me question why people are so different. I guess each car fits each driver. Reading may not be one of my tools, but drive and willpower are. They push me and guide me through all the turns on the track.

Emotionally, it is good to be driven and to push yourself, but it is just as important to know when to push the pause button and stand back and take time to look at yourself apart from your competition. This is a new lesson for me. It was a special person from my pit crew who made the point to me that you cannot drive and drive and drive and expect to be the best driver you can be. You have to get away from the race—find a setting that is opposite from the roar of the engines, a setting where you can go to find some peace, to review your current performance on the track, and to look toward future ambitions.

This has been one of the hardest lessons for me to learn. Once I got on the racetrack, it was really hard for me to get off. When I did, I was too aware of the other drivers around me. I struggled to find some inner peace. I started becoming aware of my inner thoughts when I began to keep a journal during my freshman year. First, I started writing about pleasant memories, and then I started to ask some harder questions of myself. As difficult as it was for me to hold a pencil and paper in my hand and confront my inner thoughts, writing the thoughts down made them more real. The thoughts I wrote were true feelings that I had not confronted since I had made the decision to aim for the winner's circle. I had forgotten many of the feelings I had as a child and how stupid I had thought I was. These feelings did not accompany me on the racetrack, but once I pulled over, they became a part of me again. I realize now that it is ok to have these memories and feelings because they make me the driver I am, but they must be put into perspective. Analyzing the feelings, accepting them, and seeing how they fit my racing style make me a better driver. I would recommend to all of the drivers in this race: find a peaceful place—your backyard, the beach, the countryside, even an empty racetrack—and write down your thoughts or at least examine your inner feelings.

Sometimes writing this book has been emotionally difficult for me. When I look back and remember some of the things that happened to me as a child, it is depressing to realize that a lot of the same things are still going on. There are things that I could not do in the third grade that I still cannot do today, and that I will always find difficult. Facing this fact really does not make the reality any easier, but until I began to acknowledge my weaknesses, I did not realize I had so many strengths. As I better understand my learning *dis*abilities, it is easier to reassure myself that I truly am not stupid, and in fact, have some really strong *abilities*. Until a person learns to face a problem and find a way to deal with it, he or she will always be forced to take second best.

I have learned to deal with my academic difficulties up to a point, but it still bothers me to realize that I am always going to have trouble in many areas of my life because of my learning difficulties. Even though it is difficult, it is important to realize that life is not fair. Every boy, girl, man, and woman has something unfair to deal with. Some people come from abusive homes while others have no homes at all. They may not have enough to eat. They may have no legs. They may have a terrible disease. Accepting the problems and dealing with them is difficult but necessary to achieve emotional well-being. Sitting back, taking a deep breath, and taking the opportunity to be true to yourself is good and necessary. I never did this when I was a child, and I think it has been twice as hard for me to accept my problems as an adult because I spent so much energy simply faking it when I was younger. You cannot afford to do that in America. You must face your problems head on, and not let them stand in your way or prevent you from doing the things you are capable of doing.

Before giving out the results of our first test, one of my teachers asked us to think about our reactions to our grades when we received them. He said that students usually react to a poor grade in one of four ways. One group blames someone else for the failure: *It's the teacher's fault; he made the test too hard, and my roommate kept me up all night talking.* The second group dismisses the failure as unimportant: *Well, this is not an important subject anyway, and one lousy grade won't make a big difference fifteen years from now.* The third group accepts responsibility for the grade, analyzes why the failure occurred, and considers how the next grade might be improved: *I knew I should have spent more time studying. I was not prepared for the discussion questions. I need to pay more attention to learning the theories than memorizing the details.* The fourth group realizes that they failed the test for one reason only—they are just plain stupid: *Everybody has always said I was not smart enough for college; I guess they were right. I am simply not bright enough to comprehend this material.* **I am stupid.**

The children who put themselves in this final group have already determined their outcome in education and life. This has been the hardest group for me to avoid. When I was younger I always placed myself in that last group. As a college student I still have trouble thinking positively and have to force myself to believe I *am* capable. I wonder about all of the individuals who have decided not to try college or not to try something they always wanted but to take second best. I am curious to know how many times they found themselves in that fourth category.

Teachers must not allow these children to place themselves in the fourth category. People who have trouble with academics are not necessarily stupid. In fact, they might be more creative in certain areas than most. It is important to find those areas and encourage the student to develop them. This will give the student a foundation on which to build and to continue his or her education beyond one class. It may take a little more of a teacher's time, and it is a lot to ask considering the respect teachers get in America today, but I wish teachers would try to develop *students*—not people who sit in class and simply observe what is going on but people who want to get involved and talk about what they have learned. The word *student* is usually taken much too lightly. A student is someone who will put forth more than the minimum time required by the average class. A student is a person who draws information from education and returns it to society. Teachers are faced with the challenge of nurturing and bringing forth the *student* in all of us. Unfortunately, my experience has been that most teachers do not realize that a play is going on right in front of them every day. Individuals are performing, pretending to learn. Please be aware that sometimes it is a performance. Deal with it before it becomes a habit, a way of life.

Dating is another one of those "performance" situations. I have found that being honest is not always necessary at the beginning. It takes time to get to know someone and his or her personality. The first impression is the best impression, so I don't shout out my weaknesses. I give myself a chance. If dating leads to true friendship, then it might be time to share some of these problems.

Although making friends has always been one of my strong points, I have met people through the clinic who, because of their learning disabilities, have real social problems. Some of these people have problems due to the severity and type of learning disabilities they have, but some of them refuse to meet people because of their fear of making mistakes or of being "found out." They have such terrible self-concepts that they are scared to even approach people. Their learning disabilities are not likely to interfere with making friends, but they have allowed their disabilities to seep into their social settings. With some students, the problem is a poor self-concept, while others cannot seem to put academics aside long enough to enjoy social situations. These people argue with their guilty consciences about taking time off from studying. Academically, they are A's on the Social Seesaw, but to the detriment of their social lives. They might even be using the need to study to "cwit" or give up their social lives. These are adolescents who have a background of low self-concept which has followed them through the years. Unless they face it, it will continue to follow them.

A low self-concept is hard to avoid when there are so many situations which have the potential for social embarrassment. Childhood and adolescence are filled with anxiety provoking situations; facing those situations with unique learning abilities is even more of a challenge. When I was sixteen, for example, the age when the desire for freedom and independence is all-consuming, I faced one of my most challenging experiences. Like most kids at this age, I was excited about getting my driver's license and anxious to drive my friends around. However, I was also a little scared. I knew that getting a license entailed taking a number of tests: a driving test, a written test, and an eye test. I was most concerned with the written test because it involved reading. Little did I know that the most embarrassing part of the exam would come when I was told to look into a pair of goggle-shaped optical lenses. This was the first step of my exam, the eye test, and I was excited. I had a positive feeling because I knew my eyes were ok, and all I had to do was look through this large Viewmaster. Damn! There were no pictures in this Viewmaster, only my most feared enemy—the written letter. I gasped. I never guessed that the eye test would involve reading! Oh, no! What's next? I had to face it, so I started reading the best I could. The letters were placed in nine groups of eight each. I had no idea that each group of letters was just that—a group of letters and not words. The enemy attacked and caught me again—I tried to read the letter groups as words. The first group of letters started with an X. Needless to say, my dreaded driver's license experience was living up to its potential, but not in the way I expected. I hadn't even gotten to the written part! Nobody had told me I'd have to read impossible words from a Viewmaster. I couldn't even think of a word that started with an X! I gave it my best shot though, and the examiner's fierce expression changed to one of confusion. I certainly got her attention. She probably tells stories to this day about the boy who tried to make words out of the letters in her Viewmaster. I know it's a day I've never been able to forget!

It is important to remember that people who have unique learning abilities have been fighting for dignity and against a negative self-image all their lives. Their relationships with others have been tainted by this even as they have struggled hard to keep their lives normal. I think that having unique learning abilities can be compared to the impact on a child of the death of a close relative or friend. The pain eventually goes away, but the scars remain for a lifetime. Even if people learn to deal with and accept their learning difficulties, the scars from teachers' criticisms, peers' teasing, and embarrassing driver's license tests will always remain. As the hurt heals, the scar remains to flaw the self-concept. Learning difficulties are too often associated only with academics. People sometimes forget that early childhood experiences remain a part of the person they deal with as adults. It is this flawed past that affects social growth.

I wrote earlier of my friend who fell off the Social/Emotional Seesaw. He appeared outwardly to be very open and outgoing and to have lots of friends. People who knew him felt that he was a very strong person and were able to draw strength from him. He and I were sometimes on panels together in which we talked to people about our academic troubles. I saw him as being very strong, secure, and sincere in what he said. But I found out later that he was faking this cool outward appearance. Socially and emotionally he was very scarred and in a lot of pain. Because he could not share this pain with others, he chose to take his life.

Because learning disabilities are hidden, it can be easy for people to hide the emotional scars that go with them. People who have physical disabilities are confronted by society. Their problems are obvious and cannot help but be acknowledged by society. They are watched more carefully for emotional concerns. Society more easily dismisses a learning disability as being an insignificant problem that can be overcome. With a lot of work, creative learners can make peace with their problems, but people must remember that the problems are still there, along with the scars. They cannot forget about the scars. Faking it is like putting a Band-Aid over the scars; the memory of the pain remains. They must acknowledge the past hurt and anger, and not try to deny they exist, and especially not use their learning difficulties as an excuse to quit, but use them to help understand themselves better and help understand how they relate to those around them.

I could go all my life faking it and hiding from the truth, but just as I have to look at myself every morning in the mirror, I have to face my problems. What you see in the mirror is important. If you see a person who cannot spell or cannot read well, you are looking at a handicapped person. If you see a person who is creative and has unique abilities, you are looking at a human being with potential. Facing yourself is a very difficult thing to do. I have found that it is easier if I break the person in the mirror into puzzle pieces. There are many pieces that make up the whole picture. Just because all the pieces do not fit together perfectly does not make me less whole. People without unique learning abilities also have pieces that do not fit. Being a creative learner can be so hard sometimes that it would be easier to just turn away from the mirror. Becoming whole is kind of like a mystery, a mystery everyone is trying to solve. The mystery is: How to make the pieces of a puzzle into a whole picture. Most people never completely solve the mystery, but working on it keeps people going. I have stopped hiding now. I am learning to face the person in the mirror, and I have started putting the pieces together. I know now that there is a solution to the mystery.

Part of the solution is to come to terms with your learning disabilities. Deep inside unique learners is a part of them that truly believes they are stupid. Children and adolescents have to deal with pressure from their peers and parents just like everyone else, but feeling stupid is a separate thing all in itself. It does not matter if fifty people with doctorate degrees tell you that you are not stupid, that you have normal intelligence ("you JUST have a learning disability"), if you *feel* stupid, that is an additional pressure to contend with. Sometimes you think, "I hate myself. I don't want to live anymore." You feel like you're the only one who is stupid. I know what it feels like when you have a constant drive to be best at something, and how it hurts more each time you find there is no way to become best. I think it may hurt more to believe you can because then you put more pressure on yourself than anyone else does.

It helps to realize that everybody battles those doubts that are deep inside, and it doesn't matter how pretty you really are if you feel you are ugly. The cost of drive, of always wanting to be the best, can get to you. I know that drive is what has helped me achieve all I've achieved, but sometimes I still hurt so much because I'm not the best and there is no way of becoming the best; sometimes I wonder if the emotional cost has been worth it.

I wish solving problems was as easy as the sun rising and setting each day. It would be nice if you could get up with the sun, assess your problems before noon, and solve them by sunset. It is difficult to deal with the fact that some problems are going to be around for a lifetime. It has been difficult for me to accept that I am never going to read or write or comprehend language as well as most of the adults I work with. I will never be cured. There is no easy way out of this problem. It will not go away when the sun sets. I will have to face it again in the morning. Accepting this reality means accepting the responsibility that comes with it. I must accept the challenge that has been thrown my way.

To survive and succeed, individuals with unique learning abilities must learn to use the tools they are given. We see the world differently than most people because of the way we process the information around us. This fact can be viewed as an asset rather than as a liability. Early in life we learn to be more creative than other people because we usually have to find different ways to do things. We cannot go up the ladder just like everyone else, but constantly finding ways around the "standard" way of doing things leads to inventing or discovering more creative methods of accomplishing our goals. At the top is the same goal, but the ladder may have an extra step between each rung, or we might have to find a completely different way to reach our goals. We might have to use a rope rather than a ladder. We learn to think differently. Children and adolescents with creative learning abilities need to be encouraged to think of their "uniqueness" as something that might lead them down a different path, but one that is just as rewarding. If they can utilize the unique aspects of their abilities rather than give up, they can find success.

Once we accept our weaknesses and acknowledge our strengths, there are other things we need to do to become successful. First, a creative learner should look toward the future and start planning early. Goals need to be set. Whether it's jotting down a few notes on a sheet of paper or talking things over with family or friends, it is important to clarify a brief plan or idea for success. This planning should begin as early as eighth or ninth grade—it's easy for students to get sidetracked or to put things off because there seems to be plenty of time to make decisions. When you are in the ninth grade, your senior year seems like a lifetime away. However, students with learning difficulties cannot afford to waste any time. They will have to spend a little extra time plotting their course. There are several things that can be done. The first thing for all students to do is to assess what they really want to do when they finish high school. They must carefully consider whether or not a four-year college is what they really want. School is harder for creative learners to begin with, and they must really *want* that degree to make the decision to continue their education four years beyond high school. The planning part not only helps make a decision, it also is the beginning of a fire. The beginning of their goal/plan can be seen as a single ember with the potential to develop into a large bonfire. This bonfire must be flaming by the time they graduate from high school because they will need it to carry them through a four-year college.

A desire for an education does not have to be the only factor that will affect a creative learner's decision to attend a four year college. In my case the desire to swim for a well-known university was my fire. It was the only reason I considered attending college. College and swimming went hand-in-hand, and as a high school senior, I was thinking only about how tough the swimming competition would be at a university. The fact that I might not be able to compete academically never entered my mind until just before I left for college. Swimming was my goal, my ember. Other creative learners' embers will vary. Their desire to become an artist, a TV producer, or a millionaire could be the spark that gets them going.

As a high school senior, I was intensely consumed with the idea of athletics; the fact that I enjoyed art led me to toy with the idea of majoring in graphic design. What I had not prepared myself for was the two years of core courses that all students have to pass before they get into their major courses. These core courses usually consist of basic courses such as English, math, and history. The reality of college academics was a rude awakening for me. Future goals rest on getting through these basic courses. A fire is not enough for students who have academic difficulties. One needs to be prepared to meet the academic demands.

A person cannot go into a race with only a burning desire to win. Hours and hours of preparation are required to compete with the rest of the racers. A transition plan that is started in the eighth or ninth grade will not only fuel the fire, but will also leave plenty of preparation time to find the right school and develop the necessary skills to compete on a college level. To do this, creative learners need to make a list of postsecondary schools that meet their specific needs. For instance, someone in a wheelchair would not pick schools that do not offer services for the physically disabled. This would not be good planning. Nor would it be wise for students who have academic difficulties to pick a school which offers no tutorial services. Many colleges offer specific services for students who have academic trouble, and it is imperative to research all the possibilities early by calling or writing the colleges that look interesting and offer good academic support systems and asking them to send information.

As the information comes in, students should categorize it by the criteria that is important to them, keeping in mind that the academic support system should be their major concern. When the list of schools has been narrowed, the entrance requirements must be considered. Students will need to know early which is more important to the colleges they are considering—grade point average or college board (SAT or ACT) scores—so that they can start working toward their goals immediately. As the creative learner approaches his or her senior year, then the fun begins. Students can then look at the things that really interest them—sports, fraternities or sororities, or simply how far they can get away from home. Creative learners who start this process early enough have an honest chance of achieving their goals and attending the college of their choice.

Once the decision to go to college has been made, the college of choice becomes less critical than the process of becoming college-ready. Being successful in college requires being independent and making independent decisions. Creative learners must start exercising their independence and their individuality by taking responsibility for their future. They must be allowed to explore the different crossroads, choose a road to take, make the proper preparations for the trip, and then, when the time comes, they will be ready to take off.

Parents: Life's coaches

Because I tend to think of life as some sort of athletic competition, it makes sense that I picture parents in the roles of coaches. Parents have the control to develop their children into the players they want them to be. As coaches, they determine the moves and strategies from the beginning. The future development of the player is in the coach's hands. Visions of games won, high school letters, and full scholarships are uppermost in their minds. Their ambitions are high and will only be fulfilled if the game is won.

Then the realization hits. A clumsy child, a problem child, a child with poor hearing or eyesight—a child that doesn't have the speed and strength to win a game or even to compete. A snag in the game plan. It's time to restructure the strategy, to gather in the locker-room and face the facts. They focus on the questions at hand. How do we win this game? How do we beat the odds? What can we do as coaches to have our player rise above his or her weaknesses? In the coach's game plan, this player has received a bad call. It is not fair, but they must deal with it. It will not be easy. They will have to restructure the game plan to fit the player's abilities rather than their own aspirations.

So what does a coach do? It would be easy just to tag along with the player and hope everything will eventually work itself out. The coaches could give up and bench the player so he or she won't become an embarrassment to the team; or they could devise a new game plan that will help the player rise above these difficulties and make him or her competitive.

Walking away from the game for awhile, the coaches examine their options. Which solution would be the easiest? The answer comes—stay with this player, who might compete somehow at a different level of competition. But wait, we forgot one thing. This player is a child. A part of the coaches, not a part of the game. The decision must be based on what is best for this child, not what is easiest for the coaches. The answer is easy now. The game plan (life) has to be changed to fit the player (child). The coaches (parents) have to change the gameplan and work out new strategies. For they are not coaches, but parents.

It is not right to walk away from or be ashamed of our own child. Former coaches are now parents. The new game plan is simply to love, but, to love the child for who he or she is, not who they want him or her to be. Face the facts. The child has learning difficulties, but he or she can play in this game. What is to be done now?

If the trip through life is to be successful, the parents of children with creative learning abilities must be supportive. Parents always walk a tightrope, never being sure that what they do and say are the right things. Life is particularly precarious for the parent of a child with creative learning abilities. Parents who deny there is a problem can add to the child's guilt and frustration at not living up to the parent's expectations. Parents who acknowledge the problem often feel guilty and overindulge the child in an effort to be helpful. This can make the child more handicapped than he or she is. Parents are faced with walking the fine line between ignoring the problem and doing too much, knowing that they will make mistakes along the way no matter how hard they try to do the right thing. The hard part about having a child with a learning disability is being unable to see a physical problem. A child who is in a wheelchair or wears a hearing aid or uses a cane or guide dog to get around has an obvious disability that needs special attention. Other parents empathize with the parents of such a child, understand their frustrations, and forgive their mistakes. They might overlook poor social skills, bad behavior, and poor grades in the child with the physical handicap because there is a visible cause (excuse) for the atypical behavior.

The parents of a child with creative learning abilities do not get this understanding from others. Their children are often viewed critically by teachers and other parents because their handicap is invisible. When these children get behind early in school and make poor grades, everybody's first reaction is that the child is simply not as smart as the other children. This fact in itself can be difficult for parents to accept. What is worse is when the child is obviously smart and demonstrates good thinking skills or good vocabulary skills at home but continues to do poorly in school. Then teachers and other parents tend to be critical and start blaming the parents for allowing their child to be so lazy and to get away with not studying. Unfortunately some children and parents believe this criticism, accept the laziness excuse, and give up on finding a way to help the child learn. Just as children with unique learning abilities must contend with the criticism of their peers, their parents must contend with the criticism of *their* peers: other parents.

I think it is important for parents to keep believing in and supporting their child, even when there is doubt about the cause of the problems. A mutual respect must develop between parent and child. Children need to know that when it seems that no one else believes how hard they are trying, at least their parents do. The parents and the children have to work together to deal with all the ignorance around them. In working together to educate the public about learning disabilities, a bond can develop between parent and child that is strong but not suffocating.

The parents of children with creative learning abilities will hear much negative criticism. My mom says that she has vivid memories of the first positive teacher's conference she had about me. It came when I was in the second grade and had been placed in a special school. She had been taking me to specialists from the time I was three years old, and had heard few positive statements about my abilities. These predictions had been confirmed by my teachers and my atrocious performance in school. In the special school I was being compared to other children who had learning difficulties, and, comparatively, my future looked bright. My mom has never forgotten that conference because it was the first time anyone had said anything positive about me. It gave her hope and kept her going through future conferences that weren't so positive. It was important that she never gave up on me despite all the disappointments she must have had through the years.

Learning disabilities are understood a little bit better now than when I was growing up, so parents can benefit from the fact that teachers are a little more knowledgeable and from knowing that they are not the only parents with a learning disabled child. It is very important for parents to acknowledge the problems their child is having and to try to find out exactly what is going on. The easy way out for the parent is simply to ignore that there is a reason for the poor grades and the frustration a child feels with school, but that is not necessarily the easiest way for the child. Children need to understand what is going on with them; they must not be allowed to think they are stupid. Parents need to remember that children with unique learning abilities are intelligent and need to understand the nature of their problems. Young children might not understand all the words in an explanation about learning disabilities, but they at least will understand that there is a reason for their learning difficulties other than the fact that they are stupid or not trying hard enough. Explanations should be as positive as possible, and parents and children must keep searching for and emphasizing strengths, special talents, and potential.

One of the hardest aspects of being the parent of a child with creative learning abilities will be knowing how much to do for the child. Parents must be advocates for their children, fighting prejudice and a rigid education system. It is difficult to distinguish between going to battle for a child and fighting the child's battle for him or her. It is difficult to know how much help is too much

and when to step in before the child becomes over-
whelmed. Parents need support in this area. They need
feedback from other parents and teachers about how de-
pendent or independent their child is compared to his or
her peers. Then they need to use their own judgment
about encouraging independence while providing encouragement and assistance when needed. Parents
should join a state and/or national group such as the
Learning Disabilities Association (4156 Library Rd.,
Pittsburgh, PA 15234) in order to get support from other
parents and to get correct information about learning
disabilities and the rights of parents and children when
dealing with the education system.

When I was growing up, there were no support groups
or information organizations for my parents to turn to,
so there was confusion, disagreement, and tension about
how to deal with me and my problems. After a few years
of doing everything the schools recommended and struggling to deal with my frustration at not being able to
achieve, my dad gave up on the school system and put all
of his energy into helping me focus on my strengths. It
was probably because of his constant reminders to think
positively, make goals, and work hard to achieve them
that I not only stayed in school, but also considered attending college. It also had the adverse effect of supporting my own denial of my problems. My mom continued
to concentrate on what I saw as my weaknesses. She attended the school meetings and never gave up trying to
find new techniques to help me learn. Her attitude was
that I had a problem that I was going to have to deal with
all my life and could not ignore. More than anything she
wanted me to accept my unique learning abilities; even
though my father supported my mother's efforts, he
wanted me to concentrate on other things so my learning
differences would not stand in my way. Both of my parents
wanted the best for me, and each thought their approach

was right. It was painful to both of them to watch me struggle with things, knowing how much I wanted to be perfect. It is sometimes hard for me now to look back and realize that much of the tension I sensed between them when I was in school was because they were worried about me. Each was convinced that he or she was doing what was best for me, and in a sense they were both right. Because of my dad I learned to think positively and focus on my athletic strengths; because of my mom I was not allowed to forget about my learning difficulties. When the time came for me to finally quit denying my problems, she was there for me to talk to, whereas my father sometimes still has difficulty accepting that my learning difficulties should play any part in my adult life. I was lucky. My family could have been torn apart like so many families are today, and lack of communication about me could have been a contributing cause to that breakup. However, through their strong, guiding hands, my parents gave me an inner strength that was laced with stubbornness. I hope I can do the same for my child one day. If I could look ahead ten or fifteen years, this is how I would like to think I would handle my situation if I were a parent:

I have a seven-year-old son named Jordan who is finishing the second grade. I have just been told by his teacher, Mrs. Gagne, that she wants to keep him back for another year. This doesn't come as a surprise to me because Jordan has had difficulties since entering school. Witty and carefree at home, he has trouble concentrating on anything that deals with school. I have seen his mood change from a rambunctious young boy outside the classroom to a quiet and subdued student. As his father, I have always been concerned with Jordan's attitude toward school. Now with this new information that he has to repeat the second grade and leave his peers, I am even more concerned about how this will affect his attitude in the long run. I have been told by other teachers that Jordan has difficulty with reading and writing to the point where he has only first grade skills. Mrs. Gagne had suggested earlier in the year that it would be wise to have Jordan tested for a possible learning disability.

A flashback: memories of my own difficulty with school weigh on me. I do not want Jordan to have the same feelings I had about special education. I do not want his self-concept to suffer by having to repeat a grade. I knew this day might come and have prepared for it. In a book I had written I had outlined what I felt a parent should do when faced with this dilemma. I remember stating that parents need to deal with the situation up front, being very careful to attach a concerned, rather than a negative, tone to the discussion. So this is what I will say:

"Jordan, you, your teacher, and I are here today to discuss the possibility of your repeating the second grade. Mrs. Gagne says that you have trouble in the way your brain sees and hears things. There is nothing wrong with your ears or your eyes. The tests that you took a few weeks ago explain what is going on. Now, this is kind of cool, Jordan. You see words in pictures. You have developed your own reading system. Your system is a little different from your friends', and that's why you're having trouble reading. Because you see these pictures so vividly, you forget about the words. Remember last week when I read about King Arthur to you, and you drew all those pictures for me? You drew those lively pictures of the swords and the battles and the horses. Well, that's how your brain reads stories. Which is good, if you want to become an artist. But, we want to give you the option to be whatever you want to be. So Mrs. Gagne feels we need to go back in and add words to those pictures. To do this she feels it would be wise for you to go through the second grade again. With a lot of

extra hard work and the help of a special teacher who understands about lost words, we can help you. You see, Jordan, I'd like you to be able to read about King Arthur to me one day. When I was younger, I had trouble reading King Arthur too. I had to find a special teacher who helped me learn to make my system work for me. If you give us a chance and work with us, we can teach you how to do that too. Now I want to hear what you think about all the things I've told you."

Although this sounds like a fairy tale, I feel that with the right attitude this approach can work, and the fairy tale can come true. I know I'm going to give it a try if Jordan and I ever need to have that talk.

Windowsill ambitions: Accepting the challenge

I have stated earlier in this book that a student is anybody who has the desire to learn; however, just because you attend class every day doesn't give you the right to call yourself a student. For several of my years I wasn't a student. I was a figure supported by a chair and desk with all my ambitions collecting on the windowsill outside the schoolroom. The things I wanted to learn were not within the boundaries of this room. The figure in the desk was only a shell. The true student was outside the classroom. I *was* a student, but not a student of academics. I was a great student at not believing in myself.

What changed that? What brought the real student within me to find the shell? How did my windowsill ambitions come to be reality? The answer in my case was *athletics*. I never won a medal in school. I was always last in academic competition. So I reached beyond the classroom to find my medal. I crawled through that window and grabbed onto an ambition and took off with it. I stepped back from the school and let it become second in my life. Instead of spending all of my energy worrying about school, I submerged it in a pool of water. I found gratification and success through swimming—my medal. Most importantly, I was allowed to carry that medal into a school. I began to grow in self-esteem. I had opened the window and let one of my ambitions fly into the room. The desk was no longer my sole support. My shell began to fill with self-confidence and pride. I was awakened to a new classroom. I saw not only myself, but education, as a new subject. Don't get me wrong. I had to work hard for that outside medal, and it took time to win my first race. But when I did, there was no stopping me. And there never will be.

What I did was step back from education, where I was getting no reward, and concentrated on another field where I had better possibilities. Simply getting up at five o'clock every morning brought admiration from my friends, parents, and teachers. If I never won anything, I had gained some respect for what I was attempting to do. My friends were curious and envious that I had the drive to do this. What they didn't realize was that my drive was far deeper than they could possibly comprehend. It came from being a failure for so many years. *Once I tasted admiration, it fueled the drive for success.* Success in the pool followed me into the classroom. The saying is true: success breeds success.

People who have creative learning abilities may not find success in the classroom because we do not fit into the educational mainstream. We may put in hours and hours of study time only to make a C. We have to find successes outside the classroom in order to reward ourselves and to build our self-confidence. Self-confidence is the key to success. Here are some steps I found helped me build self-confidence, and strategies that helped me cope with difficulties during the building process.

First of all, I should mention a possible flaw in this first stage of building self-confidence. I have known people who have succeeded in areas outside of school and still lack the confidence to become a true student of academics. It is a common flaw for some students to bolster themselves only on those windowsill ambitions and never bring them into the classroom. Too often when people take a step toward another ambition, they never return to the classroom. School is forgotten and dropped from their goal list. They use this one ambition as a crutch which allows them to disregard education. Creative learners must be aware of this possibility and remember that the ultimate goal is to enhance their education by building their self-confidence in other areas. They need to listen to their teachers and parents for guidance, and they can't forget their primary goal—*education.*

Second, goals must be set and a mental plan developed to meet those goals. I began this process by asking myself, What were my ambitions? How far was I willing to go to achieve these ambitions? What steps would I need to take? What sacrifices was I willing to make so that my ambitions could become reality? The answers to these questions determined my goals. Once I set my goals, I let them create their own story and guide me to success. Creative learners should never be afraid to let their goals be known to others. Hidden goals become lost dreams. I had to confront my goals. Think about them. Say them to myself and to others. I had to imagine myself succeeding. I let them become part of me. I allowed them to change with me as I grew.

Although specific goals might change, the important thing is never to lose sight of long term goals. For instance, when I was going through high school and my first year of college, my goal was to be a *great* insurance salesman. I not only told everybody this, I believed it. Whenever some information would come across the news or I would hear someone talking about insurance, I would listen. I would make myself curious about what that news was or what those voices were saying. As college went on, I found myself less interested in insurance. I still kept my mind on selling, but was not as locked into insurance. Although my specific goal changed, all those years of telling myself I was going to be great at *something* was what really counted. The Great Insurance Salesman idea got me through the first couple of years of college because it was my goal. Even though my goal changed, I always made sure I had a plan which would carry me to some type of successful achievement. If I had lost sight of my goal, I would have risked the possibility of losing the *vision* of achievement.

Taking chances and going after a goal might seem very frightening at first, but creative learners have to make themselves believe it is worth the risk. It might seem easier just to let things be and not take a chance. I could have done this. I could have surrounded myself within secure walls. Don my best clothes and lie back. Let life go on around me as if I were not a part of it. Padded with security, I would rest comfortably—but who wouldn't in a coffin six feet underground?

Building self-confidence is not easy, and does not happen all at once. As stated in *The Velveteen Rabbit*, becoming "real" takes a long time. "That's why it doesn't often happen to people who break easily, or have sharp edges, or who have to be carefully kept." Creative learners have got to realize that their academic problems are only society-made. They are guidelines that society has assigned to success. We must realize that success cannot be defined by society; it must come from within. If we cannot make it by society's guidelines, we must find another way. We must search for that certain something within us that will make us stand apart from others. It might be playing tennis, writing poetry, racing cars, hang gliding, parachuting, photography, or playing an instrument. We must find our strengths and develop them.

Then we will be ready to confront and attack our disabilities.

We can begin this process by learning as much about our unique learning abilities as possible. To do this we should find out what our exact weaknesses are and examine them. We have to learn what the problem is in order to deal with it and find a way to get around it. My advice to other creative learners is to sit down alone and write out what *they* see as their individual strengths and weaknesses. They can then go to their parents and/or a teacher or counselor and show them their list. We must learn to take advantage of the knowledge and advice of others and weave it into our own perception of our unique abilities. We are the kings not the jesters. Teachers and parents are too often willing to make excuses for us. We can't allow ourselves to take the easy way out. We must stand strong at our throne and take control of our kingdom (life). We might find that our guards (parents, teachers) will try to protect us from the cruelties beyond our castle, but effective rulers must walk through the streets and examine the problems for themselves. Only then can they find the best solutions.

It is important for creative learners to surround themselves with people who want to and know how to help them. Because parents cannot always be objective, it is important to find someone—a mentor—to talk to. This person might be a friend's mom or dad, a former teacher, a distant relative, or a school guidance counselor. People with unique learning abilities must also surround themselves with materials that can help them, such as dictionaries, spelling checks, and computers. These materials must become part of the daily routine.

My final suggestion to the person with unique learning abilities is to remember that he or she is a creative learner and, therefore, sees things differently from other people. Although this will be a problem in some areas, learning to use our unique abilities to our advantage can place us ahead of the crowd. For example, the fact that I do not think in the same logical order as most people has helped me understand some things that other people had difficulty comprehending. Sometimes in classes when explanations are the reverse of what most people expect or seem to be totally illogical, I seldom have difficulty. Many people are bothered by illogic, but nothing ever seems logical to me, so illogic doesn't bother me. It is logical for most people in the United States to turn the pages of a book from right to left. Reversing the direction to learn another language would not bother me. I might use my unique sense of logic one day to invent something so creative that people will be amazed at how I came up with such an illogical, but useful idea! I have been told that one of the people who helped invent the Macintosh computer is a creative learner. I am not surprised that one of us would come up with the idea of creating a computer that communicates through pictures (icons) rather than words. I also understand that many creative learners have become quite successful entrepreneurs because of the unique way we view the world.

Having a learning disability is not something people would choose as part of their lives. Just as it is a problem that is invisible to others, it carries with it some social and emotional problems of which others might not be aware. The important thing is for us to be aware and to learn to deal with our private pain. We must learn to confront and accept our learning differences. We can view them as a part of us that we do not particularly like, but something we might learn from to make ourselves better people. My creative abilities have made me more determined and more aware of what was going on around me. They also have made me angry at times. I still get upset and frustrated when the pieces of the puzzle won't fit. I get angry with the system because it does not fit me or make allowances for who I am and because it does not allow me an easy way out. But sometimes I feel excited at discovering a talent I didn't know I had or that my unique way of thinking solved a problem that no one else had found an answer for. As far as tools go, I could have been given worse. With my creative learning abilities, I have the potential to succeed in ways no one else could dream.

EIGHT

A New Beginning

This is the last week of the last class of the last quarter of my last year of college. The days are numbered. Graduation is near. Yesterday I turned in my final paper, and it felt good. I guess my emotions are mixed. For four years I have poured myself into my books and into athletics, not really taking a break. And now I am about to start working in the real world. Two days after I graduate I will begin my career as director of marketing for Anchor Management Systems, an insurance consulting firm. However, I am still keeping my options open. There is a creative part of me that has yet to be satisfied.

I remember leaving high school. Being scared to death of what lay ahead for me in college. The tests, the papers, the "all-nighters" all seemed too much for me to handle. I was afraid of not succeeding. However, I found out that being afraid was what helped me get through college. Now I look ahead to a new challenge. One in which money is earned instead of grades. And again I am scared. The clients, the business meetings, the presentations will be new challenges. This time though, I feel more secure, ready to take on the challenges of the business world.

In a small way I am hoping that it will be easier, that I will fall into a routine and succeed. For all of my life, school has been a struggle and the primary obstacle for me to overcome, and now it will no longer be present. What a strange feeling! I guess that's why this last week has such an aura of mixed feelings. Feelings that range from fear to excitement to sadness. The University of Georgia has attempted to be my biggest obstacle, but what

I've learned was that UGA was not the only obstacle I had to overcome. The biggest obstacle was me. It's kind of funny. All the classes I attended and all the speakers I heard and all the tests I took all seem to equal one thing—they seemed to teach me more about myself than about any one subject. Now that I look back on them, my eyes seem to be a little wider. I think I see what college is all about. It's not so much learning a profession; it's more learning about yourself. Teaching yourself to become disciplined and *curious* and at the same time focusing on ambition to be the best person you can.

Maybe this is the point of education that is hard to see until you have completed it. It's helping students find out what they are interested in and what they are capable of doing. It should give them a foundation to draw on, but at the same time give them the tools to build on that foundation. As stated in the beginning, everybody is not necessarily given the best tools to complete a job, but if taught to use the tools they have in a creative manner, they can build as fine a house as anyone.

AFTERWORD

Rosemary's Turn

Riding a One-Eyed Horse

One side of his world is always missing.
You may give it a casual wave of the hand
or rub it with your shoulder as you pass,
but nothing on his blind side ever happens.

Hundreds of trees slip past him into darkness,
drifting into a hollow hemisphere
whose sounds you will have to try to explain.
Your legs will tell him not to be afraid

if you learn never to lie. Do not forget
to turn his head and let what comes come seen:
he will jump the fences he has to if you swing
toward them from the side that he can see

and hold his good eye straight. The heavy dark
will stay beside you always; let him learn
to lean against it. It will steady him
and see you safely through diminished fields.

                                   Henry Taylor

To me all children are special, unique individuals. The joy I have always experienced in teaching was trying to figure out the unique qualities of each of my students and to help them discover those qualities in themselves. I suppose this is why I have always found myself drawn to those students who have qualities that are a little different from their peers'. Really unique qualities are not always as easy to deal with since they are unique to "special" individuals.

I began teaching in 1973 in an experimental class-room called a "pre-first grade." It was made up of twenty children who were not quite ready for the rigors of the "real" first grade even though they were of the correct chronological age. The idea of the pre-first grade was that the students would be exposed to the basics needed for first grade. Essentially, they would be given time to mature and would enter the first grade the next year without having to say they had failed or were repeating the first grade. I was given only a few curriculum materials because this classroom was a new concept. Since it was not really kindergarten or first grade, I was left to design my own curriculum based on the things I had learned as a graduate of Early Childhood Education. Not having taught before, I did not realize that most teachers used curriculum manuals and placement tests to guide their instruction. Lacking these materials, I looked to the children to begin building my curriculum. We talked and got to know each other, and their individual needs and wants were made clear to me. They had more needs and skills to learn than I could possibly teach them in one year. It did not take long to realize that the best way I could help these children was to lead them to believe in themselves and in their own power to succeed. If I could give them that, I felt they would be able to work to their potential when they encountered the regular school curriculum. That goal became the basis of my curriculum planning for that year and the rest of my teaching career.

My husband finished school the next year and we moved to another town late in the summer. The only available teaching job was a fifth grade classroom in a small rural school. Being the rookie, I was given the least desirable class—the "low group." Most of these students had failed at least one grade, and therefore were larger than the other fifth graders. Not only were these children considered to have bad attitudes, but some were on probation as juvenile delinquents. I was given curriculum manuals to teach them math and reading, but soon discovered that what the other teachers really wanted was simply for me to keep this group quiet and out of trouble. If the students learned anything in the process, that was considered a bonus. I was not as much afraid of teaching this unique group of students as I was of dealing with fifth graders. They seemed so much larger than the preschoolers I had been trained to teach that I was not sure what to do with them. I felt sure that the "Eeensy Weensy Spider" song would not maintain their attention for very long, although it would certainly make them question their teacher's sanity.

In the early 1970s, schools were experimenting with new educational models. This school was no different. Instead of having a pre-first grade, they had experimented with diversified teaching. In the mornings, all the teachers in a grade level taught language arts and math to students grouped by ability. In the afternoons, the students were all grouped together for science, social studies, and physical education. Two teachers taught science, two taught social studies, and I was assigned to teach PE. My high school PE teacher has not stopped laughing yet! I was left on my own to teach students a subject for which I had no training and no curriculum guide. I found that I was prepared. I devised my own curriculum based on the individual needs of the students. The same goal I used in teaching my pre-first graders worked with fifth graders: helping them discover and reach their potential in each subject.

During the four years that I taught fifth grade, I was always looking for some way to make each of my remedial students and each of my PE classes feel like they were the most special group of children in the entire school, because to me they were. To encourage my group of slow learners to read, write, and do math, we joined with another class to develop a fifth grade newspaper. The newspaper became such a hit that it eventually developed into a school newspaper. The next year, my principal arranged for me to have a journalism class made up of a few students from each grade. These students were not always the best or the brightest. The stipulation was that each academic group must be represented, including those who had unique learning abilities. Having no set curriculum, this class was free to explore its own special abilities. Over the eight years of its existence, *Close Encounters of the Younger Kind* became an award winning newspaper, and the class had its own radio show and local newspaper column. Some of the students who went through that journalism class are now journalism majors in college and have many accomplishments in their own right. Those students who were not the most talented writers discovered other talents and developed interests in layout, advertising, cartooning, and interviewing. There was something for everyone to do because the goal was not to develop the best newspaper, but to find the special qualities of each student so as to make the strongest news team. The students in this class not only learned to discover their own strengths, but also learned how to look for the unique qualities in the other students in the class so that those strengths could be used in the various projects. As a class, they learned how to use each student's best qualities to produce a quality product. And as the teacher, I was never bored.

By 1980 I had earned my master's degree in Reading Education, since reading seemed to be the most dire need of my fifth grade students. It was at this time, however, that I was persuaded to enter the field of special education when I was assigned to the special education class. As I look back, I realize that I had always taught children who had somewhat more special abilities than those around them. The children I had taught in the classroom had unique learning abilities and many of my PE students and journalism students were physically, artistically, and intellectually gifted. However, at the time I was a little hesitant about what would be required of me as a special education teacher since I had no formal training in this area of education. Although I immediately began to add special education certification to my master's degree, I essentially took over the class with no training.

In my first special education class, the students ranged in age from eight to fifteen, and carried labels of "educable" or "trainable mentally retarded." Most had been in this self-contained classroom with the same teacher all of their lives. Minimal attempts had been made at mainstreaming the children into art, music, and PE classes. I had been encouraged to take this class in part because I believed these children could be mainstreamed and become vital, important members of the school. I anticipated that I might encounter some resistance from other teachers who were unsure about how to deal with these children in their regular classrooms. The teachers were most accepting, however; the resistance came from within my special class. Each student had an extremely poor self-concept. They saw themselves as being very different from the other children in the school. They had always been in a special classroom away from the mainstream of the school, with separate lunch times and separate play times. They did not know how to interact with other children and were afraid to take the risks involved. We took a lot of time that first year working on things other than academics. It did not take me long to realize that these children were really no different from any of the other children I had taught. All of my students had been unique children with individual needs. These students simply had a label attached to them certifying that they were "special." My teaching goal would be the same. We would get to know each other and I would help them figure out their unique needs and strengths and help teach them to believe in themselves enough to try to achieve their potential.

I did not succeed with all of the students. Many of them had believed their labels—stupid, dumb, different, FAILURE—for too long. As hard as I tried, I could not convince them to accept new, more positive labels. Although I did not give up, I had to admit to myself for the first time that I would not be able to reach every child. The ones who would let me in, however, I could teach to soar. Special education did not offer as many day-to-day rewards as regular education, but when those rewards came, they made all the hard work worthwhile. Many students went through my special education class; eventually all were mainstreamed for all but reading and math. The diversified teaching model worked to our advantage. When the students left their homerooms to go to individual language arts and math classes, my students simply came to me to work on their individual levels, and also to work on self-concept and social skills. I am sure that some would have preferred not to have to attend any type of special class, but this arrangement seemed satisfying to most of the students and teachers. In fact, mainstreaming was so acceptable that the number of special education students had multiplied, and many of these students were labeled "learning disabled." About the time I completed my certification in Mental Retardation, I was given a group of five boys who carried the LD label. I returned to school to get my specialist degree in Learning Disabilities. I also began to entertain the idea of getting a doctorate in Special Education.

In 1985 I entered the doctoral program in Special Education at the University of Georgia. It was then that I faced my own lack of self-confidence. Although I had been a successful teacher, I could not quite picture myself as a Doctor of Education. I was not sure that I had the ability to complete a doctoral program, but after encouraging children for twelve years to risk failure, I could not simply sit at home and wonder if I could have done it. So I left the secure environment of my little rural school and my small community college to become a little fish in a big pond. Leaving my husband to take care of the house and our three cats, I lived in an apartment during the week and returned home on weekends. It was not an easy time.

Several months after entering the program I was offered a graduate assistantship in the Learning Disabilities Adult Clinic. The clinic provided evaluation and service for students at the university who had learning disabilities. Although my major duties would involve evaluation, I would also be involved in providing direct services to a few students. Christopher Lee was my first student. He was an athlete, a swimmer on the University of Georgia swim team. Before I met him I was told that he had a severe language disability and that my first responsibility would be to help him understand that he would have an extremely difficult time at the university and should consider other alternatives. Chris informed me during our first meeting that it had been his dream since elementary school to swim for the University of Georgia. My job assignment was in direct conflict with his dream. The more I tried to convince him to take an easier path, the more he convinced me that his motivation and desire to succeed outweighed the problems caused by his learning disabilities. It wasn't long before I was caught up in his dream and found myself working almost as hard as he was to see that his unique learning abilities (as he and I came to see them) did not stand in his way. As I watched him win battle after battle, our relationship developed into a special friendship.

The most difficult struggle Chris and I faced was over his unique learning abilities. He tried hard to convince me that he was having trouble writing essays because his

high school teachers had never taught him how to write.
He just needed a little more practice.

*Actually, Chris, your writing problems are based in
your language problems. The words in your sentences
are in an awkward arrangement; you leave out and
misplace words. This is a syntax problem. You have a
learning disability.*

He hated those words and made every effort to convince me they were not true. He had always been "a little
slow," he said. He thought that he probably was not as
bright as most students but he would make up for that
by working hard.

*Actually, Chris, you're just as bright as the other stu-
dents on campus. Your evaluation shows that. Not all
people have proof that they're intelligent! But you have
some deficits in the way your brain processes information. You learn differently from the other people here.
You will have to work harder, but we'll also have to work
together to find some ways to get around your deficits.
It's important for you to understand what's going on in
your brain that's causing you to have problems in your
schoolwork.*

The first quarter we worked together was very hard
for Chris because he found out that, as hard as he tried,
he could not "fake it" with me. His thorough evaluation
showed the exact cause of his academic problems. I knew
what his cognitive strengths and weaknesses were the
first time he walked through my door. I was not aware of
the strength of his internal fortitude or his desire to succeed, but I understood his disabilities. I knew that hard
work alone would not overcome them and that somewhere
down the line he was going to have to face that fact and
deal with it. For the first time, Chris was forced to deal
honestly with his learning problems. He had two
choices—to trust me to help him or to continue heading
toward dismissal. As his guard gradually began to lower,

our work times together became more and more productive.

The first thing we tackled was his writing. After working with him so long on this book, it is hard to look back to the time when he could hardly put a word on paper. His thoughts were restricted by his inability to spell the words. We began immediately to work with a word processing system. I discovered that he had an IBM PC in his dorm room, but he would not use it because he felt it was too complicated. I have found that this problem is not uncommon among students who have difficulty visually processing symbols. Using a DOS operating computer system requires entering letters and symbols such as semicolons and backslashes in certain sequences. Students who cannot easily discriminate these symbols or who tend to reverse, omit, or add symbols to sequences can become frustrated with the computer before they ever call up their word processing program. For these students, a Macintosh computer is a better choice because it uses pictures and menus and requires few discrimination or sequencing skills. The only computer available in the clinic at that time, however, was an Apple II, so I began by teaching Chris how to use the Bank Street Writer word processing program. This is actually a fine program for beginning writers. It met Chris's needs because it freed him from having to worry about the formation of letters and the spelling of words. He gradually learned to put his thoughts on paper without worrying about the spelling or the punctuation. Once he learned to use the computer, it became his major tool and classroom modification, and he purchased a Macintosh of his own. As I have worked with Chris on this book I am constantly amazed at the enormous talent and love he has for writing. I shudder to think that this may have remained hidden forever had it not been for the invention of a simple word processor. The words he writes are still woefully misspelled, but it does not matter because he knows that the final product will be in a form that he will be proud to let anyone see and read. Because word processors have become such valuable tools, our clinic now has a computer lab with several IBM and Macintosh computers so that our students can have access to them at any time.

As special as Chris is to me, he is only one of many students I encounter each day who have unique learning abilities. Right up front I'll admit that I have been accused of seeing only the positive qualities of my students. That is my preference in dealing with all human beings. So I will acknowledge immediately that these students are not perfect. Some of them miss appointments, put off assignments until the last minute, and party too much, like many college students. I tend to defend my students more than I need to because I feel that there are many people who do not understand learning disabilities or why students with learning disabilities should be in college or get special considerations. When I describe my profession to people outside of the university, I often get remarks such as "Oh, you must have a lot of athletes in your program" (actually there are very few) and "Oh, you mean those lazy students who want to get out of working for their degrees?" and "What are *those people* doing in college?" In my opinion, the students I work with stand out from the crowd in their levels of motivation and determination. Chris is one example; there are many more.

The Learning Disabilities Adult Clinic (LDAC) is supported by the University of Georgia to assist those students who have unique learning abilities. A fairly young program, it was established in 1982 by Dr. Noël Gregg, the clinic's present director. It has since grown from serving only a few students with a volunteer staff to serving well over one hundred students with a staff of three full-time coordinators and numerous graduate assistants. As a member of the graduating class of 1990, Chris is part of the largest group of graduating seniors who received assistance from the LDAC throughout their college careers.

The students I work with are all remarkable in their own ways, and their learning abilities are as unique, their needs as individualized, as they are. My job in working with them varies. I have the expertise as a learning disabilities specialist not only to participate in their evaluations but also to use those evaluations to help anticipate the academic modifications and assistance they might need. I talk to their teachers for them, and I help them learn how to talk to their teachers. The students must understand their unique learning abilities completely in order to approach teachers with confidence; therefore, much of my job is explaining over and over again their processing problems and how those problems cause them to learn in a different manner from their peers. These things are not easy to hear sometimes, and they are often not easy to understand. One of the reasons learning disabilities are so difficult for others to understand is because they involve complex neurological processes that are invisible and come with confusing terminology. My students do not always have to explain to their teachers that the reason they cannot spell is because they have problems with auditory synthesis and visual sequencing. However, they need to understand in their own terminology what exactly is going on in their brains that makes it difficult for them to read or spell or remember things or communicate their thoughts or organize their lives. Identifying the specific aspects of what is going on in their brains makes their unique learning abilities a little less mysterious. They come to understand why all their hard work over the years never seemed to pay off. They come to understand that they are not stupid. Once they understand how they process information, they can understand why some things are easier or harder for them to learn than others. They learn to deal with their unique abilities as facts of life rather than mysterious obstacles.

My students have a variety of unique learning abilities which call for unique classroom modifications. For many, the easiest modification is simply extra time. These students might take a little longer on tests to read the information because it takes them longer to decipher the visual information in front of them. The letters change around on them sometimes or their brains omit or insert words into the text. On math tests, they may need to take more time to insure that they do not misread a sign or symbol that might cause them to misinterpret an entire problem. Students who have difficulty processing visual information need extra time for the same reason as someone who is visually impaired and has difficulty seeing the material. It does not mean that these students are slower than the others in the classroom or that they are not prepared for a test.

Sometimes it helps students with visual processing problems to take their tests away from the rest of the class so that they can read the material out loud to themselves. This seems to help keep them from missing important details. Some students have such problems reading that they need to have their study materials and tests read to them. The purpose of tests is to assess whether or not students are learning the material. If a student knows all about Caesar and Cicero, but has difficulty distinguishing the two words in writing, a written test does not assess the student's knowledge of the material. Modifying the testing procedures, however, allows a student with unique learning abilities to compete on equal terms with his or her peers. For someone with this particular type of problem, the teacher might let the student take an oral test or take the same test with a reader. Our students do not want extra privileges. More than anything they would like to be just like everyone else in the class. They know, however, that in addition to having to work harder outside of the class, they will occasionally need modifications such as having to have someone read their tests to them.

Learning disabilities are characterized by neurological disorganization. Some of our students cannot get to class on time with all of the materials they need. However, the most detrimental effects of this disorganization are reflected during test-taking. The students usually know the material, but because of their inability to organize that material into easy-to-grab chunks of information, they often take longer to respond to answers on a test. This is another reason students might need to have extra time on their tests and to be allowed to take them in a private room. Students who have to talk their way through the masses of information in order to get to the correct choice need to have interactive tests. Again, an oral exam may be a good modification, but it takes a patient and understanding teacher to sit and listen to a student who needs to sort through all of the information before coming to a conclusion. One effective compromise is to allow the student to take the same exam as everyone else, but to take it with a proctor in a private testing room. While some of our students feel comfortable sitting in rooms and organizing the material out loud, others feel that they need someone with them to nod a head every now and then to give encouragement. Even though the proctor may have no idea if the student is getting the answers correct and the student knows this, it seems to help the student as the hours go by for someone to say, "I think you're doing just fine."

Chris sometimes took this interactive approach to test-taking. Rather than having me read his exams to him, he would read them to me, thus assuring that I would correct misread words. He would select an answer and explain to me why it was the correct choice. In explaining it, he would sometimes change his mind or make a note to come back to that question because he was unable to explain his choice very well. On a subject such as botany, he would become a teacher and explain all of the diagrams and how they related to the question, and I would sit and nod my head as if I understood. I was usually nodding more in amazement that this young man who could not pronounce or read these words could tell me all about them and appeared to truly understand the concepts of the subject. I believe "interactive" exams are a very valuable modification. They simply involve the process of thinking out loud, but they provide an avenue for students whose neurological disorganization hinders them from retrieving information quickly. Sitting in on these exams also allows me, the observer, insight into the students' reasoning abilities so that I might be able to make suggestions as to how their reasoning processes can become more efficient.

The most common problem we see in our students is written language disorders. Some have problems with the written symbol system, as Chris does, while others have difficulty communicating because of an inability to organize their thoughts or perceive the needs of the reader. For many of them, learning to use a word processing system effectively has become a necessary tool, and we have found that most instructors do not mind allowing the use of a computer for written assignments or tests. As with the above-mentioned modifications, the student is achieving the same goal as all of the others in the class; he or she is simply using a different manner of reaching that goal. The LD clinic is now equipped with various types of computers and programs so that students who need to take their tests on a computer can do so. We try to make things as easy as possible for teachers to make modifications, and the availability of testing rooms, readers, proctors, and computers helps. We occasionally have to do some creative scheduling, but the teachers are generally very cooperative.

There are some students whose writing problems do not require the use of a computer. These are often students who have difficulty organizing their thoughts into a coherent form. A technique I use with many of my students is brainstorming. I help them develop their ideas about a topic by asking questions and typing their responses in their own words. This helps them think through a topic and develop some themes. We then look at the printout of the brainstorming session and see what kind of organization the ideas might form. I often use highlighters during this phase to make the organization as clear as possible. Ideas that can be grouped together are highlighted with the same color. The students can then take this rough draft of ideas and work on the essay or paper on their own. Students with organizational difficulties may take hours to respond to one essay question. One of my students asks for permission to bring blank notecards into the test. She writes her ideas or responses to essay questions on the individual cards and then lays them out in front of her to try to find the most logical organization. Unless she is able to literally manipulate the information, her writing is extremely disorganized and distorts her true knowledge and understanding of the subject. Index cards are a compensation tool as valuable to this student as the computer is to Chris.

Because the learning environment is so verbally oriented, students with verbal problems are obviously at a great disadvantage. However, some students have verbal strengths but find it difficult to understand or gain information from nonverbal materials. Where diagrams and pictures help Chris comprehend verbal explanations, they only serve to confuse those who have nonverbal problems. The explanation for such differences in abilities lies in understanding the neurological foundation of learning disabilities. There are many complex theories about the causes of learning disabilities, but in explaining them to nonprofessionals, I have found that people want as simple an explanation as possible, so I have learned to give only the basics. For those who are interested in a more thorough explanation, there are many books on the subject and neurological consultants who can explain the functioning of the brain much better than I.

If you are a neurologist, you might better skip to the next paragraph because you are not going to like this overly simplified explanation. The left side of the brain basically processes verbal information and the right side of the brain basically processes nonverbal information. Learning disabilities involve processing problems which often are specific to one side of the brain or the other. The general neurological disorganization often seen in students with unique learning disabilities is a result of the "whole brain" trying to deal with the neurological aberrations on either side. We can assume that people who have difficulty processing verbal information (language, words) have a neurological deficit in the left hemisphere while those who have difficulty processing nonverbal information (usually visual information not attached to verbal symbols, i.e., diagrams, pictures, body language) have neurological deficits in the right hemisphere. There is disagreement about the exact nature of these deficits. Some professionals feel there is actual damage to the brain, although the damage is so minor that it does not show up on simple brainwave tests, such as an EEG. Recent research suggests that these deficits result not from damage, but from something that goes wrong during the actual development of the brain in the fetus. They theorize that some cells get misplaced or fail to develop as the brain is forming. This theory fits the idea of the brain appearing to work as if it had "short circuited" or was "miswired." With the advancement of medicine, the mystery of what actually goes on in the brain of a person with learning differences will probably be discovered in the near future; however, for those of us who work with creative learners and their interesting brains right now, it is important only to know that the area of the brain in which the deficit occurs reflects the type of processing difficulties the person will experience.

It is necessary to understand this only because it is confusing at times to deal with these two groups of students whose strengths and weaknesses are opposite, but who are all considered to have learning disabilities. The students with nonverbal deficits tend to have trouble with math, the sciences, and graphs in economics, while students with verbal deficits have little or no trouble with those subjects. Although these subjects involve verbal explanations, the reasoning involved tends to be nonverbal. A significant amount of math knowledge is communicated via nonverbal symbols, although the more abstract it becomes, the more it requires language. The sciences also require comprehension of charts, graphs, diagrams, and experiments. Sometimes people with nonverbal deficits also have trouble learning foreign languages because they can only comprehend it as a visual symbol system that is foreign to them. They usually rely on words and language to reason through the visual elements of their lives, and in that sense a foreign language involves nonverbal reasoning since they do not have sufficient command of the words to rely on them. Professors have been confused by these two groups of creative learners when they encounter two such students in a class. I remember working with one of Chris's literature professors. This man was more than willing to be accommodating and made a particular effort to understand why Chris had such difficulty with writing and why using a computer was so helpful to him. Chris was the first creative learner the professor had encountered, and he seemed pleased with himself at the end of the quarter because he had an understanding of students with unique learning abilities. He also understood why they would usually need some kind of modification when having to express themselves in writing. He called me at the beginning of the next quarter very confused. "This is very interesting," he said. "One of my students in my *senior* literature class just informed me that she has a learning disability. She's a *literature major*! How can this be?" The student he was referring to was indeed a literature major. She could impressively discuss Emerson and Poe, her two favorite authors, and she loved to write short stories and poems. She was verbally gifted, but as a senior, she had yet to pass her freshman basic math class. She could not reason with material that was not presented in a verbal format. The reason she informed this professor that she had unique learning abilities was that we advise our students to do this with all of their teachers, even if they do not anticipate having a problem in the class.

We have found that professors are much more understanding and accommodating if they know in advance that a student might encounter problems. Unfortunately, many of our students really want to "try out" a class to see if they can do it on their own without special attention being given them. If they wait until they fail the first test and then tell their professors that they have a problem which might be interfering with their learning of the material, it sounds as if they are trying to find a way around the "F." The literature major used the approach we advised; in the privacy of the professor's office, she told him: *I would like you to know that I have a learning disability. I don't anticipate that I will have any problems with this class, but I wanted you to know in case something comes up during the quarter that we might need to talk about.* The difficult part for the professor was that the literature major was only the second student he had ever encountered who had said the words, "I have a learning disability." Because the first student was Chris, the professor had experienced back-to-back the two extremes of students with creative learning abilities. I understood his confusion, and did my best to explain.

If anyone ever has any doubt about the motivation of students who work in our clinic, he or she will have little doubt after observing them during final exam week. The allotted time for finals is three hours. Our students are generally allowed to have twice the time on tests that other students do, so those who request extra time on their finals are usually allowed up to six hours. While few of the regular students spend their full three hours on exams, our students will quite often work furiously without breaks to finish within six hours. They do not waste or misuse the modifications they are given. I really look forward to going to the English department each quarter to take over the monitoring of the freshman English finals at the end of their three-hour period. The other students have long been finished, but the computer room is alive with energy where several students with unique learning abilities continue to write. As they have been taught to do, they make sure to budget at least an hour to proof their completed essays. I think I would be tempted to give up after writing for five hours straight, but these students have struggled too hard to blow the final exam. Exam week can sometimes be as exhausting for us, the specialists, as it is for the students. We have seen the work and effort they have dedicated to a subject to the point that we are as invested in their success as they are. However, our job is to remain calm, to promote a sense of tranquility, to lessen their anxiety. One of the most difficult exams I ever monitored was one in which I sat and smiled for five hours and whispered encouraging words as one of my students reasoned through his accounting exam. This student had asked little of me over the years we had worked together, and I knew absolutely nothing about accounting. He usually used our times together to talk about how his life was going. This quarter he had talked about how difficult it was to take a class that his disabilities interfered so much with (his deficit area was primarily in attending to visual detail, a necessity in accounting). Talking through his exams, reading every word out loud, and repeating every number as he wrote it forced his brain to attend to those tiny details it so often failed to process. I sat with him through every accounting test that quarter as he read and explained to me the reasoning behind every accounting problem. As I sat and listened for a final five hours, I kept reminding myself that I was serving an important function. I was this student's security blanket and sounding board for a few hours of his life. Being there was important to him, and for that person on that day, my function was to listen.

The nature of the unique learning abilities determines the subjects our students will have difficulty with. My student with the accounting problems always performed well in classes in which "seeing the big picture" was the major requirement. Some of our students have little trouble memorizing facts or dealing with details, but they have difficulty conceptualizing, or putting those details together to form a complete concept or theory. Test modifications do not help these students as much as one-on-one attention, or what we call academic therapy. We decided on this terminology after some debate because we did not know exactly what to call the one-on-one services we offer. We are not exactly tutors because we are not experts in the subjects we help our students with. Tutors usually approach their jobs from the point of their own subject knowledge. They often explain material in a manner similar to the professor who teaches a class. Tutors usually know from experience which parts of a subject are difficult to comprehend, and they concentrate on detailed explanations in order to make those parts more understandable.

Our method in using academic therapy is to approach a subject from the standpoint of a student's unique learning abilities. Our students usually do not need to hear the material repeated. Because they learn differently from the average student, they need a different approach. As specialists armed with knowledge of a student's cognitive strengths and weaknesses, we approach academic therapy sessions with the unique needs of each student in mind. For example, there have been quarters in which I have worked with several different students in the same basic freshman English class. Each week they all had the same assignment, but they each had different needs, and I used a different approach with each one. I am not an English teacher, but I understand the abilities and disabilities that each student has and how their unique learning needs interfere with their writing. One may have trouble with mechanics, another with organization of ideas, another with sense of audience. They have these specific problems because of their specific learning disabilities. They also have strengths, and I try to help them learn how to use those strengths whenever possible. For example, I might say: "Your ideas are excellent. Your teachers always like your unique approach to different topics. It's your organization that gets you in trouble; let's see if we can figure out a way to get your ideas across in a more organized way." or "Your writing skills are very good, you know. You write good, clear sentences, your punctuation and grammar are always correct, and you have an excellent vocabulary. The reason you're not getting your ideas across is because you're forgetting about the reader. You need to remember to always think about what the reader, or your audience, needs to know in order to understand your basic ideas."

The academic therapy needs of our students vary as

much as they do. It is the only service we provide that we charge for, so some students may be limited in the number of quarters they receive this special help. Some students use this service every quarter, while others pick and choose their times according to their specific needs. For example, a student who has good verbal abilities but poor nonverbal abilities may only need academic therapy for those quarters in which he or she is taking a math or science class. The cost of special learning services needs to be considered when students with special learning needs are considering which postsecondary institution to attend. There are many students at the University of Georgia who get caught "between the cracks." They cannot afford the extra cost of academic therapy each quarter, but they are not destitute enough to qualify for financial aid. Federal law requires that our students be allowed equal access to postsecondary institutions, but one-on-one tutoring is regarded as being beyond this basic requirement. Even though the majority of students with unique learning abilities really need this extra assistance, very few schools are able to provide it as part of their basic services. Most learning disabled college students are aware that they will have to work harder than their non-learning-disabled peers in school in order to achieve their degrees, and many of them take jobs in order to earn the extra fees required for academic therapy. It's just another example of their motivation, drive, and desire to earn that degree that will show the world that they are college graduates.

Building independence and preparing students for coping after college is one of our primary goals. By helping them understand their learning disabilities, we help them learn to anticipate possible problems and be prepared to solve them. One of my students had severe short- and long-term memory deficits, a particularly devastating deficit for someone majoring in agricultural education, a science field that requires much memorization. He spent several disheartening years struggling through the core curriculum, anticipating that the courses would get easier once he entered his major area. When this did not happen, he decided he was not college material and would have to settle for less than a college degree. He worked as a lab technician for several years, when a friend who understood how dissatisfied he was suggested that he might have a learning disability. He was tested by our clinic and discovered that he was indeed capable of college work but had deficits that were interfering with his achievement. He enrolled in school once more, willing to take a chance that the Learning Disabilities Adult Clinic would be able to help him. Richard was the second student assigned to me that first quarter I worked in the clinic. Chris and Richard remained *my* students until they graduated. Richard was a challenge not only because his learning disabilities were so different from Chris's, but also because I had no knowledge of most of the subjects he was taking. In the three years I worked with him, I became very knowledgeable about agriculture, feeling a bit lofty by the fact that I could discuss soil saturation levels, farm equipment costs, and the impact of insects on crop yields. In helping Richard devise methods of memorizing all the facts involved in his agriculture courses (from soil parts to bug parts to plant parts), I memorized these facts right along with him. We explored all possible mnemonic strategies until we settled on several that worked best for him.

Working with Chris and Richard at the same time helped me realize the different manifestations of learning disabilities more than any course I had ever had. Both students had difficulty remembering the material in their classes, but for different reasons. Chris had difficulty attaching language to the concepts he learned. He had to struggle with the language before he could begin to encode the words into his memory for later recall. Once he obtained the language, he could place the concept accurately among the other linguistic structures in his mind. He then had little trouble remembering it, at least for a short period of time. Whereas Chris's deficits in language interfered with his ability to remember, Richard's deficits were in memory itself. As a result, he had difficulty with all courses that required remembering lots of details. What Richard excelled in were his education courses, in which he was required to teach this material to others. He understood *learning* and knew that it involved more than just memorization of facts. In working with our clinic, Richard learned to understand what caused him to have trouble in his classes and how to devise compensation strategies. He learned to carry a pocket calendar with him at all times and to constantly check it to make sure of the things he was to do during the day and to write down everything he needed to remember.

Richard now works for an agricultural extension service in a rural Georgia town, where he directs the 4-H program in the schools. If he ever needs to know a plant or bug part, he can refer to one of the many books distributed by the extension service. He often writes or calls to tell me about all the things he is doing with "his kids." He wrote the other day to tell me that he had found a videotape on mnemonics and planned to use it in one of his 4-H units this year. "I'm afraid I'm still forgetful at times," he wrote, "but I guess I'm glad I've had some tough things to do in my life because that's how you find out they're usually worth the risk."

More and more students with learning disabilities are taking risks. They are deciding to pursue postsecondary educations, and they are succeeding. To be successful, however, they must be properly prepared. I make the following suggestions based on my experience in working with Chris and other students who have the potential to succeed in college but whose unique learning abilities will require special considerations:

1. Planning for college should begin as early as ninth grade and should be a team effort involving the student, parents, and teachers or school guidance counselors. The student and the parents will be responsible for the student's needs after high school, so they need to share in the process of planning for the postsecondary years. Teachers and guidance counselors should be resources in providing suggestions and advice, but the student and parent need to pursue this goal as a team, assuming more and more responsibilities as the student progresses through high school. Beginning early will assure that the most suitable postsecondary institution is chosen and that appropriate college preparatory courses are taken during high school.

2. Either *Lovejoy's College Guide for the Learning Disabled* or *Peterson's Colleges with Programs for Learning-Disabled Students* should be purchased. These guides give specific information about the services offered for students with learning disabilities at postsecondary institutions across the United States. The student should select a number of possible institutions and send off for information using the suggestions in the guide for questions one might wish to pursue regarding the program for students with learning disabilities. After receiving responses, choices can be narrowed to a few institutions and arrangements be made to visit them. Parents and students should make an appointment to visit the special service center and ask if it would be possible to meet some of the other students with learning disabilities on campus to talk with them about the attitudes of their instructors toward special-needs students and about the services they receive from the service center.

3. Parents need to plan ahead for the extra expenses education will require. College is an expensive proposition for everyone, but for students with special learning needs, special considerations may mean extra expenses. Some students may find that the services that will best meet their needs are only available at private colleges or colleges that are specially designed for students with learning disabilities. Even in public colleges, the special services for students with learning disabilities may involve some extra costs.

4. If the high school curriculum does not emphasize study skills, the student should work with a tutor or take a community college course to learn strategies for taking tests, reading textbooks, and organizing time. The students I have worked with who have been most successful are those who enter college knowing how to study and who can enforce a study schedule upon themselves. Disorganization is one of a college student's worst weaknesses. As a freshman, every student enters an environment where everything is new and unstructured. Simply getting around campus can be an ordeal at first. Students with special learning problems need to be prepared to handle new situations; unfortunately, the opposite is often true. Students who have been in the special education system have often learned to look to someone to take care of problems for them. Independence needs to be encouraged throughout high school if the student expects to find success in college.

5. Self-confidence is one of the greatest motivators and is probably the deciding factor between those students who let their learning disabilities defeat them and those who defeat their disabilities. Whether college is a consideration or not, every high school student with learning disabilities needs to find something outside of academics in which he or she can be successful. This may be sports or a hobby or a part-time job. Research has shown that most successful adults with learning disabilities attribute some of their success to having a mentor or a series of mentors who guided them at different points in their lives. Parents and students should explore mentor possibilities—someone in the community who might take a little extra time to teach skills such as photography or mechanics, or a hometown hero who understands the importance of motivation and self-confidence in a young person's life. The mentor might even be a teacher the student had in an earlier grade, someone who could be both objective and concerned. Mentors can provide the adult advice that children will not seek from their parents (since all teenagers know that parents don't know anything). Parents and students need to consider one final answer for building self-confidence: Coping with learning disabilities can be very stressful and anxiety-provoking, and counseling may be needed to help the child deal with his or her special problems. It is important to seek out a counselor with some experience and understanding in dealing with learning disabilities. If possible, the student should consider joining a self-help group made up of other students with learning disabilities. Self-confidence is difficult to achieve and even more difficult to maintain, but it can make all the difference in a student's success in college.

6. In addition to working on self-confidence, students with learning disabilities need to spend time in high school learning self-advocacy skills. In the postsecondary environment, these students will be totally responsible for their needs. There are people and agencies available to assist college students with special needs, but the students must be aware of these resources in order to know who to contact. They need to become aware of their rights as adults with learning disabilities and how to fight for those rights if they are ever discriminated against. They need to learn appropriate social skills because they may have to approach professors to ask for special help or special considerations. These are skills that need to be taught before the students enter the postsecondary setting.

7. During their final year in high school, students with learning disabilities should have a thorough college-oriented evaluation. They need to understand the exact nature of their disabilities and gain some understanding as to how those disabilities might affect them in the college environment. They will meet challenges in college that they never faced in high school, and they need to be prepared as much as possible. Some college learning disabilities programs require current evaluations before admission to their programs, and some, like ours, conduct their own evaluations. If an evaluation is a requirement, arrangements should be made early in the senior year so that there is time to work on those weaknesses, such as writing or study skills, which may prohibit college success. If an evaluation is not required, arrangements should be made to have one through the school system or a private psychologist who will agree to concentrate on college concerns.

8. When the time comes to take the Scholastic Aptitude Test or other college entrance tests, the school guidance counselor should be notified and special arrangements should be made. People with learning disabilities are allowed to have modifications on these tests, but special dates and different testing sites are often required.

9. Students need to be equipped with the proper tools before they leave for their new college adventure. Every student should have a good college-level dictionary and thesaurus. Depending on a student's unique learning abilities, he or she might also need a computer, word processor/typewriter, a computerized spelling checker, and/or a good calculator. A pocket organizer might also be useful, but the student might prefer to wait on this until getting to school. Many colleges sell organizers that are sprinkled with relevant school-related information such as final exam dates, school holidays, preregistration, etc.

Entering the college environment having made all of these preparations makes students' battles easier to win. They will have to endure four or more years of studying harder than anyone else, seeing special tutors, asking for special modifications, and struggling with grade point averages that do not reflect their time and effort. They risk emotional burnout before their dream is realized. They will need support, but they can get through. One of the most pleasurable aspects of my job is helping my seniors work on their placement files. I help them write their resumes and gather letters of reference. This is sometimes difficult for me because I feel that I could write the most convincing reference letter. I would like to have the chance to tell an employer how dedicated, disciplined, creative, and hardworking my students are, a fact I know from having watched and worked with them for several years. Those of us who work with these students at the clinic see a side of them that few people ever see. We have shared their joys and disappointments and know their inner characters better than most of the people around them.

I cannot write those reference letters because most of the students do not want their prospective employers to know they have learning disabilities. They need to make their way in the world just like everyone else, with determination, creativity, and skill, just as they made their way through college. I simply feel privileged that I have been allowed to be part of their lives.

APPENDIX 1

Regents' Essay
Topic: Describe Your Favorite Piece
of Furniture

An Empty Stool

My favorite piece of furniture is a stool that sits in my room. The stool stands two feet high and is about two feet wide. It could probably be described as a box with legs. The top of the stool opens and shuts leaving storage space in the middle. This is not just any old stool. It has personal value to me for many reasons.

Perhaps the reason why this piece of furniture means so much to me is the fact that I built it with my own hands, and it was the first thing I ever built. In the second grade I participated in a workshop and chose to build a stool. After finishing the stool, I brought it home to show it off. I was very proud of my accomplishment. It is strange how this stool that once was a piece of wood with no particular form or shape made me so happy. It gave me my first sense of accomplishment.

Another reason the stool is my favorite piece of furniture is the fact that it has been with me throughout my life. The stool was a big part of my younger years. For instance, I used the stool as a hiding place. Through the years I kept everything from toy trains to dirty magazines in it. The stool was a place where I could lock away my childhood secrets. The stool went through the physical changes of childhood just as I was going through them. I painted it different colors as I grew older and my tastes changed. The last change I made to the stool was to glue newspaper articles all over it. The articles were about things I wanted to do or be one day. It seemed right that my goals should become part of the stool. As I got older the stool seemed to become more sturdy as I became more mature. It seemed as though we were both going through the same phases of life together.

Now I'm at college while the stool still sits in the corner of my room at home. Torn newspaper articles hang from it, and there is an empty space inside waiting to be filled again. Time seems to have pulled the stool and me apart, for I am at college filling myself with knowledge while my stool is home empty. I guess it is true that things lose their value as time moves on, but the stool is till my favorite piece of furniture.

APPENDIX 2

Sample Essay Not Using Computer Freshman Year

What I an today is what I was yesterday. Each day I am influenced more and more by the different things around me. School, religion and the environment where I live, all have an effect on how I grow and search for the ferson who is inside me. But to me my family and may friends are the two major influences that have made me what I am.

My family has always been my strong point in life. Each day that goes by, each hour I'm away from them I become and strong and more indepandent. When I was younger my parents brought me up with a free mind. A mind that should be left open to hear every side of a story. When ever my parents and I would get into a fight, they would always sit down and work oith me on it. This has shown me that I could just sit down and talk about their problems. Another strong point my parent gave me is that every-one is epual in life know matter what problem they might have. For example. two day befor coming to Georgia last quarter. I met a girl who had been deformed since birth. When I wa first introduced to her I was stung. I could not belive this sad sight I saw in front of me. I begun to fuill sorry for the lonely person. But after I left I begun to thind that everyboudy nust alweys fill sory for her. Which is wrong, people should be treated and look apond in the same way. For this way of open minede way of think I thank my parents.

Frinds have alway had had a stron infulences on up

since I have been young. To me there ae good friends and bad friends. which I have learned from both. For example I had a friend named Mich when I was in forth grade. He was the school buly, you could say, he alway acted like he was your friend. Until he got around people hoow he like more. this taght me nnever to treat anyone like they are trash. But I've also have had great frends. That have tough me the meaning of fun, careing and trust. To these friends I tamk.

My environment has been has been change a lot both with school and friends. But know matter if its sunny or even pouring down rain. I wouldn't want to be in any other enviroment.

APPENDIX 3

Journal Entry, Freshman Year

There's not a cloud in the sky as I look out my open dorm window. The sun is shinnig bright and ther seems to be a frishnes in the air. Today my mind is cluderd. I have so many imotions ready to burst out and scream. The small amount of greenery on the trees seem to simolize the amount of peace I feel inside. Traffic is light, and there are only a few runners jogging by. There is one small lady walking by my window. I've seen her around a lot, her name is Rachel and she the ohnly girl migge on campus that I have seen; I seem to run into he a lot. She alway seem so happy. But I never see her walk with other peop. I'm sure she has fiends but I'm also sure she a lone. Last night i walked down this road that lies in fornt of me. I was a lone. For the first time. I finnally figurd out my problem. I have lots of friend but it doen't seem to matter any I can't get close to them. I not a lone. I see other people that have the same sickness I have, such a Rachel. The trees will evenchaly blum out to be full and strong. I hope I will.

APPENDIX 4

Journal Entry, Freshman Year
(cursive writing sample)

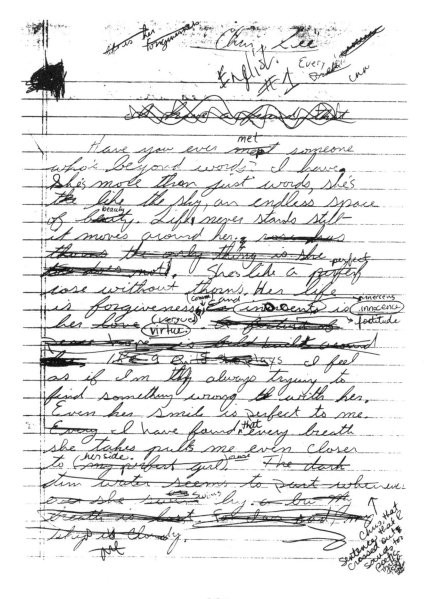